Seven Goddesses
of the
Hellenistic World

© Amy Griswold

About the Author

Jo Graham is the author of two previous books on Pagan spirituality, *The Great Wheel* (Llewellyn, 2020) and *Winter* (Llewellyn, 2020), which address the crisis of 2020 as part of a historical pattern the Etruscans identified as the Saeculum and discuss how we may respond to it based on our understanding of the cyclical nature of time. She is also the author of twenty-seven books, including the critically acclaimed works of fiction *Black Ships* (Orbit, 2008), *Hand of Isis* (Orbit, 2009), and *Sounding Dark* (Candlemark & Gleam, 2021).

She has worn many hats in her life, including professional lobbyist, executive director of a national LGBT+ organization, mother, partner of nearly thirty years, foster parent, teacher, Guardian ad Litem, and author of educational materials. Her spiritual practice is eclectic but increasingly focused on the Hellenistic world and its deities. Find her online:

@jograhamwrites (Twitter) and JoGraham (Patreon).

Seven Goddesses

OF THE

Hellenistic World

Ancient Worship
for
Modern Times

Jo Graham

Llewellyn Publications
Woodbury, Minnesota

FIRST EDITION
First Printing, 2022

Cover Art by Faryn Hughes
Cover design by Shannon McKuhen
Editing by Laura Kurtz
Interior art by the Llewellyn Art Department

Llewellyn Publications is a registered trademark of Llewellyn Worldwide Ltd.

Library of Congress Cataloging-in-Publication Data (Pending)
ISBN: 978-0-7387-6726-0

Llewellyn Publications
A Division of Llewellyn Worldwide Ltd.
2143 Wooddale Drive
Woodbury, MN 55125-2989
www.llewellyn.com

Printed in the United States of America

Other Books by Jo Graham

The Great Wheel: Living the Pagan Cycles of Our Lives & Times (Llewellyn, 2020)

Winter: Rituals to Thrive in the Dark Cycle of the Saeculum (Llewellyn, 2020)

Dedication

For my father,
who kindled in me a love of the ancient world.

Contents

Introduction

If you were able to go back in time to visit one of the great temples of the ancient world such as the Parthenon or the lost Serapeum, you would be awed by the beauty and majesty of it. The choirs, the incense, the offerings, the hundreds of people gathered for rites—today, these observances are distant memories. Few of us will ever be part of anything like that.

However, the great goddesses of the Hellenistic world were often worshiped more modestly with more intimate rites at home shrines or small temples. While we cannot reproduce the rites today, we can reach for the emotional content of them. The deities who inspired them can be present in our lives today, even if we do not have the trappings of ancient and beautiful temples or great civic rites.

Seven Goddesses

In this book, you will meet seven of the great goddesses of the ancient world, specifically the universal goddesses widely worshiped in the Hellenistic world between 320 BCE and approximately 200 CE. During this five-hundred-year span, their worship flourished across the Mediterranean and beyond. You will meet seven goddesses, each chosen because they reached out to a wide variety of worshipers over a long period of time rather than being confined to a particular people and place and because they continue to be relevant to many. For example, a goddess who concerned herself primarily with fishing might continue to be relevant to fishers but would be of limited interest to most people.

Some of them will be familiar to you: Isis, Athena, Aphrodite. Others will be less familiar: Atargatis, Tyche, Cybele. One, Epona, is most familiar today as a Celtic deity; her worship also spread across the Hellenistic world, which is the context we will explore. In ancient times you would have first encountered goddesses organically. If you had lived in one of the great cities: Palmyra, Alexandria, Pergamon, Cyrene, Syracuse, or even Marseille, you would have heard their stories as you grew up. Different places might have emphasized worship of a different deity, but all of them would have been known in a vibrant polytheistic society.

The question of how they were worshiped is complex and not of a single piece. Archaeologists and historians are continuing to discover new material and new information. However, asking how these goddesses were worshiped in the Hellenistic world from 300 BCE to 200 CE is a bit like asking how Christ has been worshiped from 1500 CE to 2000 CE! By whom? Where? When? Even in the same city at the same time are multiple churches with very different teachings and rituals, and when you expand your examination to cover millions of people over five hundred years, generalizations become misleading. Do Christian worship services use incense or candles? It depends on who and when. What roles do Christian churches allow women? It depends on which churches and when. The Hellenistic world was no different. There were vast differences of time and place. There are many reconstructions of ancient worship based on different information which are contradictory but not inaccurate. If one version of a story or a goddess or a set of correspondences doesn't match another, that doesn't mean one of them is wrong. Just as someone growing up Catholic in Italy in 1550 would have an extraordinarily different view of Christianity from someone growing up Quaker in Pennsylvania in 1800, so too did people in the Hellenistic world have widely different experiences of Pagan religion. I am not attempting to present a definitive portrait of worship or indeed a reconstruction of the worship at some particular place and time. Instead, I hope to provide a window into that distant world so like our own.

First we will encounter each goddess through a story, just as you would have if you had grown up in one of the great cities of the past. Then we'll examine the story and its context through journaling and reading. Then we'll delve deeper with a meditation directed at meeting this goddess in a modern context. We do not live in the Hellenistic world, so we cannot recreate the past. Hopefully this book will make these ancient goddesses relevant and alive to the modern polytheist. Lastly, we will provide a modern rite to each goddess appropriate to a solitary practitioner or a small group.

To optimize your use of this book, you will need a means of journaling whether it is a physical book or an electronic journal.

You will also need some specific ritual equipment for the rites, including candles and incense if you use it. It is worth mentioning specific items that were widely used in the Hellenistic world across various deities which are not necessarily a part of modern Pagan practice. Again, some people use them and some don't, another illustration of variation!

One of the most common ways to honor the gods was to pour a libation, an offering of wine, water, or another liquid while declaring that it is for them. Sometimes libations were elaborate, but more often they were simply the tipping of a few sips from one's own glass with a simple benediction, such as "May Tyche favor us." Most of us have pitchers and cups or glasses we can use for this purpose. If you wish to be more evocative, you may acquire a two-handled cup, the style most commonly used in the Hellenistic world. If you are doing a rite outdoors, you may pour directly onto the ground. However, then as now, people didn't like pouring wine onto their floor! There was a libation bowl (sometimes made of silver or another precious metal but more often painted pottery) that one poured the libation into. After the rite, the libation bowl was emptied outside onto the ground. If you would like to acquire a libation bowl for your use, there are many reproductions available online, or you may simply use a large bowl that you like.

Another very common way to honor the gods in the Hellenistic world was by burning incense. This is still a common mode in modern Pagan practice, so you may already have an incense burner and be familiar with different kinds of incense. I've suggested incense for each of the goddesses mentioned. If you do not use incense for personal reasons, feel free to skip it. Likewise, I will suggest other ritual accoutrements specific to each rite. Feel free to substitute if some things are not available or you do not use them, e.g., substitute a piece of fruit for a honey cake if you are vegan.

In ancient times, goddesses were worshiped at altars. In temples, altars were very elaborate stone or fine wood tables sometimes placed outside, where fires could be lit or offerings heaped beneath large statues. Anything of that scope is beyond home worshipers, so when I refer to an altar I mean a surface that you are using as a devotional space. It may indeed be a table, the top of a bookcase or cabinet, a mantelpiece, or any other surface in your home that is handy. Some modern pagans have a permanent altar set up—for example I reserve the top of a small cabinet in my office for this purpose. Others only set up an altar temporarily in a space which is usually used for other purposes, like a dining table. Either is fine. If you are using a space normally used for something else, just move the everyday things off and put them back after you are done.

Many modern Pagan traditions open ritual space with calling the quarters, or invoking deities or elements to seal or cleanse the space. This was not an aspect of the ancient worship because calling on the particular goddess to request her attention hallowed the space in itself. Therefore, none of these rituals incorporate quarter callings. Only the goddess you are working with is called, and no further protections or cleansings are necessary.

Each of the goddesses in the following chapters had many aspects and was worshiped in different ways at different places and times. In each section, I have concentrated primarily on one aspect so that the story, meditation, and rite are coherent. However, what is presented here is by no means definitive! For example, I have concentrated on Aphrodite Pelagia, Queen of the Sea. If some other aspect of this goddess speaks to you more strongly, please consider what appears here a stepping-off place to spur your own inquiries and research.

I have selected which stories to tell and aspects to emphasize in order to present a balanced picture; in other words, not all of them are mother goddesses or all warrior goddesses. You will assuredly encounter some stories you had not heard before or aspects that surprise you, and that's part of the pleasure. There was never a strict orthodoxy. Then as now, Pagan worshipers varied greatly in what they did and how they believed. If something doesn't match what you have read or studied, that's fine. Different things were celebrated at different times and places. For example, the worship of Isis was widespread for at least four thousand years over the breadth of a continent. There is no singular correct or universal way to worship her or tell her stories. I have chosen to present a telling appropriate to Hellenistic Alexandria, which is only one of many ways to tell a story that was cherished by so many.

Read on and join me in this journey!

Chapter One

Why the Hellenistic World?

The majority of people who have ever lived on earth were pagan. That is to say, when we look at the full range of human cultures across the globe for the last ten thousand years, most people practiced polytheistic religions that we would now call pagan. As we look at religious practices ancient and modern, there are three kinds of deities: gods of place, gods of peoples, and universal gods. Let's explore each one.

Gods of place are perhaps the oldest type. Prehistoric peoples were struck by natural places that seemed holy or numinous—perhaps a mountain that looked like a giant face when the sun set behind it, a spring that rose clean and pure in the middle of a rocky and forbidding landscape, or a cave that seemed it might lead to the center of the earth. These places became the earliest foci of worship and gradually became associated with specific gods and goddesses. Covered in chapter 5, one example is Atargatis, who may have begun as the river spirit of the Euphrates River. While some of these deities became more widely worshiped, most gods of place remained strongly associated with the sacred landscape they inhabited.

Locality-based worship represents a problem for both ancient and modern worshipers: What if you live a hundred miles from the sacred spring that speaks to you? What if you live a thousand miles from the mountains that form your sacred landscape? Humans have always been mobile and for this reason, gods of place usually welcome those who come to the place, dwell in it, and respect it. Some sacred places around the world have been considered holy sites for thousands of years. Many different people have lived in these sacred places. Who they are and where they came from is secondary—what is important to gods of place is that they are there now and part of the life of these special places. The peoples' appearance or genetic heritage isn't important. If people leave permanently, they are no longer part of the place and usually no longer of interest to the gods of place who inhabit it.

The second type are deities of people. Most of the gods we think of as Pagan deities were of this kind—part of a particular culture and patrons of a particular people with a distinct cultural identity and genetic background. They were Hittite gods or Celtic gods or Aztec gods or Scythian gods. They belonged to a people whom they championed, often at the expense of other peoples. Some of these religions are widely practiced today. For example, Judaism has cultural, genetic, and ethnic components to it as much as it is simply being about attending certain religious services. The same is true of Hinduism and many Native American and African religions.

Here is where the issue of cultural appropriation arises. If you are not of a certain people, born into a particular ethnic, genetic, and cultural milieu, can you worship these gods? Do you have a right to practice these customs? Do the gods even want you? There is considerable controversy within these faith traditions about who really belongs, controversy that is opaque to outsiders. For example, many dozens of books have been written discussing the question of who is a Jew and if it is possible to convert to Judaism at all or under what conditions. Do you need genetic Jewish ancestry? What about children who were raised by Jewish families but are adopted? What about children who were raised in another faith but have Jewish ancestry? What about people who practice Judaism as a gentile spouse but have no Jewish ancestry themselves though they will have Jewish descendants? All the nuances of these subjects are the source of constant discussion within the community. Someone simply declaring they are Jewish and believing themselves able to define Judaism is considered offensive by most Jews.

These issues are also present with other religions. If you are drawn to a deity in a living religious tradition that is not part of your heritage, you must tread very carefully. Every group has rules about who can enter and who can't, under what circumstances they are welcome, and what they must believe and do to be part of the community. Some welcome converts and some do not. Respect requires that we follow the rules of communities we wish to join. These questions do not arise when we are talking about religions that existed long ago in cultures which are no longer living. There is, for example, no living Sumerian community which can be offended.

Universal Gods

So where does this leave us if we are not drawn to the religion of our birth? Are we simply defined by our genes? Must everyone worship the gods of their genetic ancestors? These questions are not new, and the answer is no. From these considerations arose the idea of universal gods and universal religions. Universal gods and universal religions welcome worshipers regardless of their background and do not discriminate based on a person's genetic ancestry. Religions of this type arose long ago in the cultural blending of the fourth century BCE. We tend to think of universal religions as being monotheistic, but that is not necessarily true. The seven goddesses in this book welcome worshipers regardless of ancestry or heritage. First, let's investigate how universal religions became established.

Buddhism, the Oldest Global Religion

Sometime around the fifth century BCE, a sage in northeastern India named Siddhartha Gautama (later known as the Buddha) began to teach what he referred to as the Middle Way, a religion that embraced the idea of treading a path between indulgence and asceticism. It taught that altruism was necessary for happiness and that being good was not weakness but greatness. The five precepts of Buddhism are based on not hurting others, behaving with compassion, and refraining from self-harm. At the time, these teachings were a thunderbolt—most other religions at the time taught that war was noble, killing the weak was acceptable, and slavery and rape were simply parts of life. At best, one had a responsibility to one's own people, one's polis, one's tribe, or however one defined one's folk; destroying or enslaving other people was good. Every group was rightly pitted against every other group. Even Greek philosophy made a distinction between people and barbarians, with barbarians being those who didn't speak Greek. Honor and fairness applied only to those who were also people. Non-people deserved nothing.

The other completely new concept that Buddhism introduced was the idea that anyone could join. Whoever you were, whoever your parents were, whatever your caste or color of your skin or ethnic heritage, anyone could become Buddhist and be equal in the eyes of the faith. Everyone was equal, even slaves or people from lower social classes—everyone! Buddhism taught that people should be judged based on their actions, not on their birth. Moreover, everyone was truly welcome. If you were willing to live according to the Buddha's teachings, you belonged. The idea that people could choose their beliefs and identity rather than being born with it was a radical shift, a complete departure from the norms of the time.

While at first confined to the area in which Buddha taught, in the fourth century BCE it began to spread much more widely. By the reign of Chandragupta Maurya (around 321 BCE), Buddhism was becoming a major religion in India and spreading to other parts of South Asia, on its way to becoming one of the world's great religions, practiced today by more than 520 million people all over the world.

However, Buddhism was not the only faith to emerge in this period that was universal, meaning that it was not confined to a particular place or people, and which reached out to converts from diverse backgrounds. Let's look at some of the reasons why an area of the world from the Mediterranean to India was fertile ground for universal religion at that time.

The Hellenistic World

The Hellenistic world was not an empire. Alexander the Great briefly ruled an empire that encompassed part of it, but it only lasted about ten years. After his death, his empire splintered into many kingdoms called the successor kingdoms ruled by his relatives and friends. While some scholars use the term "Hellenistic world" to refer only to these states, most mean the greater sphere of cultural influence, of interconnected states that tied together by trade, language, culture, and competition that covered an area far vaster than Alexander ever ruled. Moreover, the Hellenistic world and its culture lasted longer than the states themselves as political entities. Even when large parts of the Hellenistic world were conquered by Rome, they maintained their cultural identity, including their gods. Indeed, all the religious practices covered in this book were exported to Rome. Rome conquered, but it did not dominate the cultural exchange. Therefore, we are talking about a period from 323 BCE to the third or fourth century CE, a span of five or six hundred years. Even today, the influence of this culture is felt in the modern West, with many people familiar with the gods, stories, art, and literature of the ancient Greek and Hellenistic world.

The Hellenistic world was quite simply a vast area of trade and contact where Greek was spoken. Just as English is spoken in many places around the world for business, education, and entertainment that are not part of the United Kingdom or have English as the official language, Greek was in the same position. The Hellenistic World was not an empire governed from Greece. It was an area where Greek language and culture was influential, one that comprised many states and many people. Just as today one may find someone who speaks English in areas far from England or find people who enjoy English-language movies almost anywhere in the world, in the Hellenistic world it was possible to find Greek speakers, books written in Greek, and business contracts and coinage in Greek over a wide area.

For example, thousands of documents attest to the robust trade between the Mediterranean and India. The Mauryan Empire, which comprised most of the Indian subcontient as far east as Bengal and as far west as modern Afghanistan, was absolutely part of the Hellenistic world, with a great deal of travel back and forth as well as considerable two-way cultural exchange. From the introduction of rice in Mediterranean cuisine to the war elephants used in Greece, many things came from India. In fact, the war between the Greek Seleucid kingdom and the Mauryan empire ended in a treaty that included, among other things, Chandragupta Maurya providing Seleucus with five-hundred trained elephants in exchange for marriage with Seleucus' daughter Helena.

To the south, Hellenistic ties stretched deep into Africa. Egypt was a Hellenistic kingdom to be sure, but the kingdom of Kush to the south was absolutely part of the Hellenistic world with trade routes that stretched from Sri Lanka to Italy. They minted coins in a hybrid style that showed the conventional profile portrait of their rulers as Hellenistic kings did, but with the inscriptions in their own language.

To the west, Cyrene in modern Libya and Carthage (until its fall) were major states in the Hellenistic world. Marseilles in France was a Hellenistic city, as was Histria in Romania on the Black Sea to the north. All the area between these points, the majority of the Mediterranean, the Middle East, and the Black Sea regions were a variety of Hellenistic states with ever-changing borders and constant trade and cultural exchange.

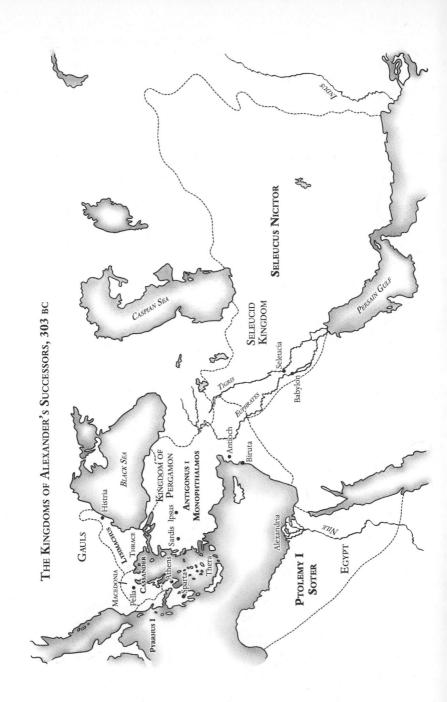

THE KINGDOMS OF ALEXANDER'S SUCCESSORS, 303 BC

SELEUCUS NICITOR

CASPIAN SEA

PERSIAN GULF

SELEUCID
KINGDOM

Seleucia

TIGRIS

Babylon

EUPHRATES

Antioch

Biruta

KINGDOM OF
PERGAMON

ANTIGONUS I
MONOPHTHALMOS

Sardis Ipsus

BLACK SEA

Histria

GAULS

LYSIMACHUS

THRACE

MACEDONA

Pella

CASSANDER

Athens

Sparta

Thera

PYRRHUS I

Alexandria

NILE

PTOLEMY I
SOTER

EGYPT

INDUS

To ask, "What does a person who speaks Greek look like? What is their race and ethnicity?" is like asking the same today about someone who speaks English. If the only thing you know about a person is that they speak English, where are they from? Australia? The United States? Costa Rica? Germany? South Korea? Do they live in a country where the majority of people speak English, or do they speak English as a second language? What is their ethnicity and religion? You can't know. Even if you added the piece of information that they currently live in New York, that tells you little. What do they look like? What do they believe? Who are their ancestors and what are their attitudes? It is as meaningless to make assumptions about the residents of Alexandria as it would be about people in New York today. The Hellenistic world is a vast, polyglot society made up of many different states, people, and beliefs rather than an empire or a single culture.

Syncreticism

The Hellenistic world was an incubator for universal cults. If you and your neighbors do not share a single ethnic heritage, ancestral language, or set of unifying stories, you are part of a syncretic culture. But before we talk about religion, let's talk about rice.

Rice had been a staple food in China and South Asia for thousands of years before the Hellenistic period, yet was not common in the Mediterranean. When Alexander the Great's armies went east, conquering Persia and getting into the wars between Indian states just before the Mauryan period as allies of one kingdom or another, they ate a lot of rice. Moreover, many of the ten thousand marriages that Alexander dowered between his soldiers and women they met in the campaigns were between Macedonian and Greek soldiers and women from Persia and India. Ten thousand weddings means ten thousand couples and ten thousand women emigrating to the Mediterranean with their customs and recipes. They wanted rice. They were used to cooking rice and serving dishes with it—they were going to have rice. Moreover, as soldiers retired and as their families grew, so did multi-ethnic neighborhoods. Women shared recipes. Families shared food. People opened little carry-out stands in Alexandria, Damascus, and Cyrene. People ate dishes with rice and liked them. Within twenty years, the sea trade between Egypt and India involved tons and tons of rice annually. The Mauryan emperors taxed the export of rice. Entrepreneurial farmers began growing rice in Egypt. Every rice dish you think of as Mediterranean—every stuffed grape leaf and pan of paella—is a product of this rich mixing.

Just as people shared food, they shared ideas. Picture these immigrant women, these military wives from a dozen ethnic and religious backgrounds cooking together, teaching young children together, birthing one another's babies, caring for disabled husbands, despairing of wayward teens together, worrying about politics and the prospect of war. They didn't just share recipes. They shared beliefs. They shared stories. They shared prayers and magical charms. They shared gods.

What did their children hear? They heard stories from many cultures. They were exposed to many different gods. There are ten thousand marriages that we know of, and many more we don't—how many children did they produce in the next twenty years? How many of those children married one another?

Let's imagine it's 280 BCE. It's been forty years since your grandparents settled in Alexandria. You are a quarter Macedonian from your maternal grandfather, a soldier of Alexander. You are a quarter Persian from the woman he married on campaign. You are a quarter Greek from your paternal grandfather, a soldier from

Ionia who joined Alexander's army. You are a quarter Sindhi from your paternal grandmother. What is your ethnicity? What is your cultural heritage? What is your religion?

The answer is the same as it is for many people today: it is what you choose it to be. Perhaps there's one part of your heritage that speaks to you most, but more likely your customs are syncretic. You put together the pieces of your heritage in ways that are pleasing and seem to fit you. Maybe you celebrate a certain holiday the way one set of grandparents did. Maybe you wear certain jewelry because it reminds you of your mother or your grandmother. Maybe you pray to a certain god because your grandfather always made sacrifice to him. You are free to choose among a variety of paths in a cosmopolitan world and gravitate to beliefs that welcome people regardless of their appearance or ancestry. Do you want to worship somewhere your friends aren't welcome? Where one of your parents isn't welcome? Where perhaps your spouse isn't welcome? The appeal of universal gods is easy to see.

Serapis, the Constructed Unifier

We will take as an example Serapis, perhaps the first god who was "constructed" specifically to bring people together. In the decade following Alexander the Great's death, one of the cities he had founded, Alexandria in Egypt, grew enormously under the rule of Alexander's friend and general Ptolemy I Soter. Populated by the baggage train of Alexander's army, veterans he invited from as far as the Sind, Egyptians who thought that the new city offered economic opportunity, and Jews who were drawn by the religious tolerance offered, it grew to perhaps 25,000 people in a very short time.

Fifteen years or so later, Ptolemy faced the problem of too much diversity. When there are too many groups with competing customs and moral beliefs, how do you ever reach social consensus? How does every difference not turn into conflict? He was a wise man who knew there were two courses he could take as a ruler: impose strict laws everyone would be forced to obey which would elevate some groups above others, or create civil mechanisms that would cross boundaries and create shared experiences. He understood that the former option would engender resentment, which would continue to fester and eventually cause uprisings. Ptolemy therefore undertook a series of steps toward the latter. For example, Alexandria had a civil constitution that laid out the same penalties for offenses regardless of the ethnicity or religion of the perpetrator. It had a city council elected by districts so that each ethnic neighborhood was represented and city courts that elected judges by district as well.[1] It also had schools that admitted boys of all ethnicities (and girls too, within another generation).

Because all of the people represented except the Jews were polytheists, Ptolemy had the inspired but simple idea of adding a god who would be the god of everyone. Each pantheon could welcome a new face. Then everyone would have one shared center of worship, one shared set of ceremonies and holidays, and one shared focus for new customs. Ptolemy said that Serapis came to him in a dream with this idea and asked Ptolemy to bring him to Alexandria. Whether one believes this was revelation or just good policy, it was very effective.

---

1. Justin Pollard and Howard Reid, *The Rise and Fall of Alexandria: Birthplace of the Modern Mind* (New York: Viking Press, 2006), 53–54.

In fact, this was the same policy enacted by the young United States in 1789. The first president, George Washington, created the holiday of Thanksgiving as a shared ritual for his new nation. While harvest festivals had been celebrated by many groups at different times, Washington thought that a national day would bring together people of English, German, Dutch, Scottish, Polish, Jewish, Afro-Caribbean and other descent on something everyone could agree on—thanking whatever form of god they prayed to for the harvest and for the good things that had happened to them and their family that year. Eighty years later, in the next era of national crisis during the Civil War, Abraham Lincoln once again declared Thanksgiving Day a holiday. While it was celebrated in the intervening years, the official date for Thanksgiving that we know today was set by Franklin D. Roosevelt during yet another national crisis, the Great Depression. Each leader sought to unify people in a troubled time. Over the last two hundred-plus years, a vast frame of custom has developed around Thanksgiving as it has welcomed each new wave of immigrants. It is the only holiday that almost all Americans celebrate.

Just as George Washington reached back to a rosy, mostly imaginary past in which freedom-loving Puritans were saved by friendly Native Americans, so too did Ptolemy reach back to mythic origins to organize the worship of Serapis. Some modern scholars attempt to paint Ptolemaic Egypt as a nineteenth-century colonial empire in which Europeans oppressed a less technologically advanced native population, but that would be imposing a modern frame of thinking on a much more complicated situation thousands of years ago. Egypt, the state Ptolemy had just become ruler of, was older and more technologically advanced than Ptolemy's native Macedon. Mathematics, astronomy, medicine, and other fields of science were far more developed in a population with a much higher literacy rate. Additionally, the Macedonians were not conquerers—they had liberated Egypt from a period of Persian rule in which Egyptian customs were suppressed and harsh foreign laws imposed.

One of the things that had caused the greatest rage among Egyptians was the Persian killing of the Apis bull. It was believed that Osiris, god of the dead, chose to take an earthly avatar in the form of a perfect black bull known as Apis. This bull was judged the best and strongest, and it lived in a sanctuary barn and paddock with its mother and other cows brought for breeding. When the Apis bull died of old age, he was mourned in the same way as a pharaoh with seventy days of funeral rites. The tombs of the Apis bulls at Saqqara have dozens of occupants, each lovingly buried with their inscribed names and dates. Once the deceased Apis bull was laid to rest, the call would go out through the kingdom for a black bull calf of perfect conformation born the day of the Apis bull's death. When he was found, he and his mother would be conveyed to Saqqara with great celebration that the god had returned.

When the Persians occupied Egypt, they slaughtered the Apis bull as a symbol of the superiority of their gods. Modern excavations of the tombs show that one bull from this period "died while yet a calf," and the next one is missing, matching the Egyptian record that says the Apis bull was killed and feasted upon by the Persians. The tombs also show an elderly bull that died in the sixth year of Ptolemy's reign, presumably instated as the Apis bull shortly after Alexander liberated Egypt; from there, the sequence of bull avatars resumes.[2] Ptolemy and the Macedonians were therefore already associated with restoring an important religious observance associated with Osiris/Apis.

Serapis was thus to be a fusion deity who combined the Egyptian Osiris/Apis with the Greek Hades, two gods of the underworld each married to a sacred queen who brought renewal to the world, Isis and Persephone respectively. Serapis would rule with Isis as lord of the riches below, of the grain in the granary, as the harvest lord. One of his most potent symbols was the cornucopia from which flowed an endless supply of bread and fruit. As the harvest lord, he shifted the emphasis away from the riches to be had in the afterlife to the plenty available today. In other words, while Osiris focused on the tomb, Serapis focused on the here and now, wealth given away freely and enjoyed rather than prepared for the grave. Serapis was thus much more in keeping with the values of non-Egyptian subjects of the Ptolemaic Kingdom, who did not have thousands of years of tradition of building incredibly elaborate tombs. Indeed, while Ptolemaic tombs certainly exist and have been explored by archeologists, they are modest compared to the pyramids or the tombs in the Valley of Kings.[3]

In honor of this new god, Ptolemy I constructed a beautiful temple in Alexandria called the Serapeum. Some travelers considered it one of the most magnificent places of worship in the ancient world. For six hundred years it was a centerpiece of life in the city. Once a year, the devotional statue of Serapis was brought out to "kiss the sun" in a parade in front of the populace. It is likely

---

2. Aidan Dodson, "Bull Cults" in *Divine Creatures: Animal Mummies in Ancient Egypt*, ed. Salima Ikram (Cairo: American University Press, 2005), 86–88.

3. Pollard and Reid, *Rise and Fall of Alexandria*, 41–43.

that the rite was emblematic of Osiris/Serapis' return from the underworld.

The Serapeum was also a technological marvel. It may have used magnets and cutting-edge engineering to create displays unlike any other in the ancient world.[4] Today, little of the Serapeum remains except for a granite Roman triumphal column raised in front of it by the Emperor Diocletian.[5]

The Universal Cults

Most of the gods whose worship spread across the Hellenistic world were originally the gods of a specific people who welcomed newcomers and had a broad appeal.

Let's take Aphrodite as an example. Originally she was the Greek goddess of love. Love knows no boundaries. Love makes no distinction of origin, ethnicity, or gender. If anyone can love or be loved, then Aphrodite can be anyone's goddess! Aphrodite was conflated with many different love goddesses who already existed, as love by any other name is still love. We therefore see conflations with her and the Middle Eastern Ashterah, for example. The goddesses already had much in common, so it was easy for worshipers in the polyglot trade cities along the coast to consider Aphrodite and Ashterah as simply different names for the same goddess. In fact, Aphrodite may originally have been imported to Greece and have been a name for Astarte, or alternately Ishtar.[6] It may have

---

4. Jean-Yves Empereur, *Alexandria: Jewel of Egypt,* trans. Jane Brenton (New York: Thames & Hudson, 2001), 24–25.

5. Nicholas J. Saunders, *Alexander's Tomb: The Two-thousand-year Obsession to Find the Lost Conqueror* (New York: Basic Books, 2006), 92.

6. Barbara Breitenberger, *Aphrodite and Eros: the Development of Erotic Mythology in Early Greek Poetry and Cult* (New York: Routledge, 2007), 13.

been that she was simply returning to her roots, as it were, by once again being conflated with these goddesses hundreds of years later.

Additionally, Aphrodite picked up attributes and epithets. For example, *Aphrodite Pandemos* means "Aphrodite of All People," while *Aphrodite Nymphia* was invoked for weddings, her epithet meaning "Bridal Aphrodite." She was also a sea goddess, invoked as Aphrodite Pelagia, a patron of seafarers and safe voyages. Sometimes she was also conflated with a ruling woman who had a reputation of being very beautiful. For example, Arsinoë Aphrodite recognized Arsinoë II, Queen of Egypt (ca. 278–268 BCE) as an aspect of Aphrodite perhaps originally because she was a generous patron of Aphrodite's temples, in addition to her reputed great beauty and deification in Egypt.[7] Aphrodite had dozens of epithets and versions of local worship because of her wide appeal.

While each of these goddesses began as the god of a particular people, they became universal gods, transcending ethnicity to be the gods of anyone who wanted to worship them. Today, they still welcome worshipers regardless of birth or blood.

I invite you to explore seven of these universal goddesses, meeting them first as you would have if you lived in the Hellenistic world—through their stories. Remember, a single story is simply an interpretation of a vast body of myth and belief. It cannot encompass the entirety of culture and experience. This is merely an introduction, a sip from a very deep well. Come and taste.

7. Elizabeth Donnelly Carney, *Arsinoë of Egypt and Macedon: A Royal Life* (Oxford, UK: Oxford University Press, 2013), 99–101.

Chapter Two

Tyche, the Trickster Goddess

Tyche, known to the Romans as Fortuna, was one of the most popular goddesses of the Hellenistic period. It's not clear where her worship arose, but it had spread throughout the Eastern Mediterranean by the third century BCE. As a patron of commerce and shipping, Tyche was especially beloved in great trading centers such as Damascus, Beirut (Biruta), Pelousion, Alexandria, and Palmyra. She is a trickster goddess—"fortune is fickle." She gives her gifts and then withdraws them, perhaps capriciously or not. Winning and keeping her favor was the subject of much art, wooing her as though she were a *hetaira*, one of the educated courtesans who were independent rather than belonging to a man, unlike many women in the period. In addition to herself, Tyche also owns you with her ability to raise you to the heights or dash you to the depths. Let's meet her with a story of the Hellenistic world, a story of the dangerous years right after the death of Alexander the Great, when all was reeling and reforming in the wake of upheaval.

Story: Lady Luck

Once there was a young gambler, and his name was Arganthos. He was lean and dark and beautiful. Perhaps he had been a soldier, for his hair was just growing out of being cropped for a helmet when he came to Antioch. Maybe he'd served Perdiccas or some other great Companion, but when he came to Antioch he had no armor, just a good knife and a broken-down horse, the kind you find when no other remount is available. Now this was in the fourth year after Great Alexander died, and there were many such, but Arganthos took care of his horse as though it were Bucephalos himself, and he found lodging at a good tavern and asked if there were any games of chance. There are always such, and many pleased to point a newcomer in their direction.

He found himself at a party held by rich men, or men who wished to be thought rich, where his handsome face and his chiton of embroidered silk from Babylon recommended him. He had ivory dice, and he let them be examined all around the table before he made his first cast. The pot was small and the wine was good, though Arganthos made certain to drink it well-watered. A drunk gambler makes mistakes, and he was never drunk when he was working.

Still, it was a good Bactrian red, and three hours and however many cups later, the room seemed hot and bright, though he could not say the same for his luck. He was just about even. He'd best leave the table soon before he came to regret the entire matter.

"Come on now," his host said. "One more round."

Arganthos pushed a coin to the center and threw again: a two and a one. "Dogs!" he said and leaned back laughing as his host drew in the pot. It was definitely time to leave. He had no luck tonight.

"Maybe your luck's about to change." He looked up. She looked down, a beautiful hetaira in a flowing chiton of lavender, that pale expensive imitation of Tyrian purple. Gold blossoms hung from her ears and gold blossoms linked together adorned her neck, dipping low between her breasts as she bent over and said in his ear, "Bet it all."

Her hair was ruddy copper, and her scent was heady. Bemused, he pushed all his winnings to the center. "All or nothing!" he said.

She smiled, her lips wide, a spattering of freckles on her cheeks, her eyes golden hazel. "Fortune favors the bold."

"Then be my lady luck tonight," he said.

Her smile widened. She bent and picked up his dice, held them to her mouth and blew on them, whispering something too low to hear. The rest of the players hooted and laughed, and she handed them back to him.

"All or nothing," Arganthos said, and threw.

Double sixes.

There was a roar of laughter. "I guess she is your luck," the host said.

"Let it ride," Arganthos said. "Anybody?" Bets were placed. Her hand was on his shoulder. He threw.

Double sixes.

"Let me see those dice," one of the other players said.

Arganthos handed them over. "I'll throw with yours," he said. "Let it ride."

Double sixes.

He looked up at her amid the clamor. "What's your name, darling?"

"Tyche," she said.

He smiled, because that was the kind of name girls took when they were working. "You're my luck tonight," he said. "What will persuade you to sit here beside me?" He was asking her price, and they both knew it. There was silver and gold enough on the table to satisfy any whim.

She leaned very close to his ear. "Bring me joy. Take me to the edge and please me. I like your face and I like your heart."

"Anytime," Arganthos said, and wiped a sheen of sweat off his forehead.

"Win," she said, and sat down beside him, her leg against his.

Double sixes.

"Are you cheating?" the host said.

"Give me any dice you like," Arganthos said. "And you throw with mine."

Double sixes.

When he left the table, he was a rich man. Well, perhaps not rich, but he had more money than he'd ever had in his life. Tyche stood up with him, her beauty a shield against the grumbles of the losers. "Come back to my lodging?" he said.

She took his arm. "Come to mine," she said, "Or you'll get nowhere at all tonight without a broken head. Tomorrow morning take your horse and go. There are other cities, and there is no more luck for you here."

He was drunk on winning, drunk on her, and perhaps a little drunk on Bactrian red. "Will you come with me?"

"I'll be wherever you are," she whispered.

He supposed her rooms were in some better house in the town. He could never find them later, but they were an oasis of delight with hanging lamps of Persian bronze and glass and a bed with red embroidered stuff and pillows in every shade. He laid her down and pleased her, his head clearing as she cried out her pleasure, taking time with no thought for his need. She was beautiful and she knew this dance. To see her clench her hands at the top was sweet, sweet satisfaction.

When her eyes opened, bright and fierce, it was like being in a vast, tender storm. His head swam and his body reeled, seeking and seeking and then spinning down into darkness.

He woke in broad daylight lying on straw in the stable beside his horse. His bags were packed and full of his winnings, and he stumbled to his feet. He was sure he'd left his bags in his lodging … he was sure he'd stayed with her … and yet here he was, his horse regarding him philosophically with his bags and his winnings.

"Tyche," he said. "Tyche." His dice were in the pouch at his side, a faint scent of incense clinging to them.

He rode out of Antioch before noon and didn't stop that night. The next day he was in another town. Children were begging at the gate with an old woman, and he gave them each a coin from his winnings, enough for bread for several days. "I like your heart," she had said. Lady Luck favors the generous.

He found another tavern, and there was a man he knew, a man he'd seen in the ranks long ago. They shared a roast fowl, but Arganthos paid. "Down on your luck?" he asked, and the man told him. It was a long story of ill-fortune, and at the end of it Arganthos put six coins on the table. "Call it a loan," he said. "One veteran to another."

"You won't regret it," his friend said. "I swear."

"No need to swear," Arganthos said. "But if you happen to know of a game around here. ..."

He won back twice what he'd given away, though no copper-haired beauty attended him. He could almost feel her at his back, a hunch telling him when to bet.

And so it went. Sometimes he felt Lady Luck with him and sometimes not, but the more wealth he gave away, the more he won. When he bought his meals, he left a generous tip. He paid for his fine clothes without haggling, and more than once gave good coin to a soldier's widow in the market square.

In Sidon he was in a game with genuinely rich men, merchants who traded all over this Inner Sea from newborn Alexandria in Egypt to Tarsus. It all came down one last throw, and he took the dice and held them to his lips, imagining hers there. "Lady Luck, be with me," he said, and breathed on them.

Double sixes.

He won a ship from a merchant of Pelousion and traded up and down the coast, learning that shipping is just another form of gambling. The ship was lost three months and he gave the captain's daughters their dower portions, brought them into his own house, and kept them as a kinsman. Then the ship made port, its cargo safe and worth a small fortune. They ran to their father with kisses, and Arganthos bought two more ships.

He married the captain's eldest daughter and doted upon her. He bought an orchard when she craved apricots while she carried his son.

Now the game was big. Kings and Companions cast dice for empires, and Arganthos cast dice with the governor of Biruta who held the town from Seleucus.

"Put your ships in the pot," the governor said, "Three grain ships. I've a desire to go in the grain trade."

"Done," Arganthos said, because he felt her behind him, Tyche with her hand on his shoulder. He threw, and he won.

"One more," the governor said, "I won't let you stop now." He had the look of a man who is in the grip of some madness. "Your ships and my money. On the table, now."

"Gladly," Arganthos said easily, and the men around the table drew their breaths, while he leaned back against his couch carelessly, as though he bet a fortune every day. "But what have you to put up? I've already cleaned you out."

"Biruta," he said. "Seleucus doesn't care who holds it. I'll resign in your favor if you win, which you won't."

"Done," Arganthos said again. He felt her, you see. He knew she was there. "Lady Luck, favor me," he whispered, and breathed on them.

Double sixes.

As he looked out across the great curved sand, the perfect harbor though Biruta was little more than a village, Arganthos closed his eyes and let the sea air fill him. Light and salt, warm and clear, these were the sounds of home. And these people, fishers who had been here a thousand years and widows of Issos, veterans and camp followers, Canaanites and Persians, Carians and Lydians, all the riff-raff of the world blown like chaff to this little town—oh, this could be home.

And it was, of course. He raised a statue in the new market square at his own expense, Tyche with her foot on the prow of a ship, a secret smile on her face as she lifted a cornucopia from which flowed an endless jackpot of golden coins. Traveler, it is there to this day.

Questions to Consider

Now that you have read a story about Tyche, take out your journaling materials, either paper and a writing implement or an electronic means of journaling. It's time to consider your reaction to the story you just read.

- What is your immediate emotional reaction to Tyche's story? How does it make you feel?

- In ancient pagan traditions, stories of a young man who wins a goddess's favor are common. What do you think Tyche likes about Arganthos? Why does she choose to favor him?

- What do you think of Tyche herself? How is she benevolent? Is she a goddess you would be comfortable invoking? Why or why not?

- Were you familiar with Tyche before? How does this portrayal of her in the Hellenistic world fit with what you expected? How is it different?

- Have you heard the phrase "fortune favors the bold?" How do you think this describes Tyche, who was known to the Romans as Fortuna?

Ancient Worship: Tyche

Images of Tyche from the Hellenistic world abound. She was an extremely popular goddess whose worship was widespread. Many of her statues were what were called votive statues, meaning that they were given to her by a donor as thanks for the good fortune the donor had received. The statue that Arganthos dedicates in the story is an example of this. Votive statues might be large, made of marble and stood in public places in a city, or they might be small and meant for home use. One example we could consider typical is known as the Tyche of Antioch. She is standing with her foot on a personification of the Orontes River, since Antioch was a river port. She's holding a sheaf of grain in her hand because grain was Antioch's main export. On her head is a crown that resembles the city's walls, symbolizing security. This statue was sculpted around 300 BCE by Eutychides and is now in the Vatican Museum in Rome.[8] It is also important to note that this statue was not originally plain white marble. We only think that classical statues were unpainted because in most cases the paint has worn off over two thousand years, leaving only the marble beneath it. However, contemporary people would have seen them as the sculptors intended in bright and lifelike colors.[9] Tyche would have originally been painted; perhaps her robe was purple, the grain golden in her hand, and the mounting waves of the river blue. Different votive statues depict her with various objects depending on the economy of the place in which it was raised and the donor's desires. Grain is common, as are cornucopia, ships, and cascades of gold coins.

Like Justice, Tyche was also sometimes represented blind-folded, to symbolize luck's blind nature. Another symbol of Tyche's capriciousness were dice. In the Hellenistic world, our familiar six-sided dice were commonly used for gambling; one very popular game seems to have been a lot like craps. This is the game Arganthos plays in the story.

8. "Tyche of Antioch," Museum of Classical Archaeology Databases, retrieved January 6, 2021, https://museum.classics.cam.ac.uk/collections/casts/tyche-antioch.

9. Matthew Gurewitsch, "True Colors," *Smithsonian Magazine*, July 2008, https://www.smithsonianmag.com/arts-culture/true-colors-17888/.

Tyche's worship was fairly simple compared to many other ancient rites. She was generally presented with gifts at one of her votive statues on special days, such as the date of the founding of the city or a date of special significance to the donor or owner of the statue. The statue was sometimes embellished with flowers, usually a wreath placed on her head. Other offerings such as wine, fruit, cakes, and flowers, were presented solemnly and the goddess was thanked for the good fortune the city or the individual experienced. Sometimes she might be petitioned for good luck. An individual might make an offering in hopes of gaining Lady Luck's favor or her assistance with a particular endeavor.

Meeting Tyche: A Meditation

This meditation may be done in two different ways: Find a partner to read it to you and take turns doing the meditation, or simply read it in a quiet place or even record it and play it to yourself.

You will need a quiet place where you won't be disturbed for twenty minutes or so. You may play soft music if you like. If you have music you normally use while meditating, you may certainly use it. If you would like to use incense, consider one of the recommendations in the list of correspondences at the end of this chapter.

Take a deep breath to help you relax. Then take another. Now begin either reading to yourself or having the meditation read to you. If you are having it read to you, close your eyes. Otherwise, read aloud slowly so that you have time to absorb the words.

You are at a big party. It's crowded, full of beautifully dressed people. Maybe it's somewhere elegant, a grand hotel, or maybe it's an awards presentation such as the Oscars or the VMAs. Maybe it's the MET Gala or the Cannes Film Festival, or simply an elegant party. You're perfectly dressed for it. You look absolutely your best, whatever your look of choice is. As you walk through the crowd, people are greeting you delightedly. There are no cold shoulders here. Maybe you recognize some people, or maybe you don't, but either way everyone knows you. Everyone is eager to shake your hand.

You walk down the red carpet. You can hear reporters commenting on how fantastic you look, how original, how distinguished, how amazing your work is. When you enter the main area of the party, people welcome you. Maybe they're old friends. Maybe they're people you've dreamed of meeting. In any event, nobody is small or jealous. They're genuinely happy to see you. They make an aisle toward the center of the room.

At the end of the aisle is a woman in a royal purple dress. Her hair is styled beautifully. She's glittering with golden jewelry. She's smiling and waiting for you. As you reach her, she stretches out both hands to you, taking yours as her smile grows. "It's good to see you," she says, calling you by name.

"Tyche," you say. "Fortuna."

"You are my guest," she says. "You are one of the fortunate ones. Tell me how you got here." She invites you to tell her how you have excelled, how you have been generous, how you have been lucky.

She invites you to tell her about the breaks you are thankful for. Maybe it's that you met someone who helped you or someone you love. Maybe it's that you had a certain job or that you had a certain teacher. Tell her. Take some time to tell Tyche what good fortune you are grateful for. Savor the good results of it. You are *lucky. You are blessed with good fortune. Tell her about it. Thank her for anything that truly was the result of pure luck.*

When you have finished thanking Tyche for her blessings in the past, she smiles and embraces you. "I am glad for you," she says. You feel her arms around you, the warmth of her hug. She is delighted that something has made you happy. "Tell me," she says, "what would you like a touch of golden luck with in the future?"

Think well before you answer her. She does not like mean-spirited requests, nothing like "I want my boss fired so I can have his job." She does not like things that hurt others. "I want my mother-in-law to die so we can inherit her money." She does, however, like generous requests. "I want to make more money so I can help my parents out financially." "I want to go to medical school so I can help people who have cancer." She also likes requests that require excellence. "I want to be the best dancer/basketball player/social worker that I can possibly be."

Then ask her for the break, the stroke of luck that will turn the tide. Remember, you must put yourself in a position to receive her bounty. You will not get into a school you don't apply to. You will not get a job you aren't remotely qualified for. You will not find the love of your life if you never talk to anyone or take a chance on anyone. Ask her. "Gracious Tyche, please grant me some of your luck in X."

If your request is pleasing, she will smile. Then she will let go of you, and you will stand there a moment in the glow of her approbation. Know that your wish has been heard. Perhaps it will be granted and perhaps it won't, but you have been heard and known. You are one of Fortuna's favorites.

Let the party fade around you slowly. Slowly you will return from this place into your own physical reality.

When you are fully back, open your eyes if they are closed, and turn off any music and put out any incense. Think for a moment about your experience. What did it feel like? How do you feel now?

Lessons from Tyche: Being Lucky

Now that you've read a story about Tyche and done a meditation to meet her, let's talk a little bit about her gifts, about being lucky.

Be Generous

As we saw with Arganthos in the story, Tyche likes generosity. She does not like selfishness. When you give generously of money, time, emotional resources, or expertise, it is pleasing to her. Every time Arganthos gave money away, he received more. When he was generous to people—his fellow veteran, the captain's daughters—what he received was their friendship and love. The old stories have bad words for those who do not give, like "skinflint" and "miser." To be ungenerous is to be churlish. Whether with money or time or love, giving freely invites Tyche's favor.

I have been very lucky in my life. I've had some amazing breaks. All of them were because I was kind to someone. All of them were because I was friendly to a stranger, welcoming to a new person, or helpful to someone who needed it. I left nice comments on the fanfic of someone who turned out to be an editor. I offered a ride home in the rain to a new member of a club who turned out to be my love of thirty years. I took time at a Pride celebration to talk to a stranger who was hired six months later for an important job and hired me as his deputy.

If you want to be lucky, be kind.

Take a Chance

You can't win if you don't play. It's that simple. You don't win the songwriting contest you don't enter. You don't get the job you don't apply for. You don't marry the person you never went out with. Too often what keeps us from being lucky is that we never took a chance.

There's an old joke about this very matter: Once there was a man who was very religious but also not very well-off. He prayed every night to win the lottery but never did. Finally, when he'd prayed for twenty years, he said, "Lord, what do I need to do? I try to be good and worthy, and yet I've asked you to help me win the lottery for twenty years and I never win."

This time the Lord answered. He said, "It would help if you bought a ticket."

Lots of people have an inner script that says something like, "Oh, I'll never get in anyway. I'm not really good enough. I couldn't possibly have done it." Well, you can't possibly have done it if you never tried. If you don't buy the ticket to your dream, you can't possibly win.

As we saw in the story with Arganthos, he kept making choices that allowed him to win. He tried new things. He gave people a chance. He let hope rule. Nothing ventured, nothing gained. I have seen how true this is in creative professions. So many people don't achieve their goals not because they're not as good as people who do, but because they don't keep taking chances. Maybe things will work out or maybe they won't but there is only one way to be absolutely certain of something not happening: don't play. You can be 100 percent certain of not publishing a book you don't send out or not getting into a school you don't apply to. There are always plenty of people who are happy to tell you that you can't win. If you listen to them, you will wind up with nothing.

If you want to be lucky, be daring.

Be Willing to Lose

Nobody wins all the time, and nobody is always lucky. You have to be willing to lose in order to win. Not every application will result in admission into a school. Not every job application will result in being hired. Every manuscript sent out won't be bought by a publisher. Every person you date won't be someone you love forever. You have to be willing to lose your bet.

Losing hurts. Rejection is painful. People aren't always kind in return. Things don't always work out. You have to be willing to hurt. It's how you respond to losing that defines you. In the story, Arganthos's first ship was missing at sea, a tremendous investment and a huge financial loss. What did he do? Did he rail against fate? Try to find someone to punish? Tell everyone that it was the captain's fault and that the captain was incompetent? No, he took the captain's daughters into his own house and treated them like family. When the ship was found, they were grateful. Indeed, one of the daughters had come to love him, and they married and had a family together and were very happy. Arganthos turned losing into winning through his own response.

When I was in my twenties, I worked very hard for my first job in politics, taking an unpaid internship that was grueling while also working full time on a night shift. After months, I got an interview for a paying position with a campaign consultant. I did the interview, and then the would-be boss said, "I'm going to be up front with you. I've already decided to hire the woman I interviewed yesterday."

I could have said some really awful things about wasting my time or stringing me along for an hour as if she wanted to hire me when she'd already decided. But I didn't. I thanked her for her time and said that I was sorry to hear that because I would really have enjoyed working for her and thought I would be a great fit. I shook her hand, said I hoped I'd have the opportunity to learn from her in the future, and went home and cried.

The next day she called and offered me the job. Her first choice turned it down. I was the clear second choice because of how I handled the rejection. I worked there two years, learned the ropes, moved on to a more responsible job, and had the break into politics that every intern wants. I was lucky that the other person turned down the job. But the reason I got it was because of how I lost.

If you want to be lucky, be willing to lose.

A Rite to Honor Tyche

This is a rite to honor Tyche and to bring a little luck into your life. This rite is designed for one person alone, but it can be adapted if you wish to do it with others.

You Will Need

- An image of Tyche/Fortuna. You may have a statuette or the like as they are commonly available, or you may make or draw your own. You may also simply print out an image.
- Fice or a die-shaped charm (if you have more than one person, you will need one each)
- A gold, yellow, or white candle

- Incense and a burner, preferably frankincense, myrrh, sandalwood or patchouli
- A small pitcher of wine or fruit juice
- A goblet or cup
- A libation bowl

Optional Extras

- A piece of fruit—peaches, figs, or apricots are ideal
- A rich cake—a mini cheesecake, a piece of baklava, or some other small cake
- A plate for food offerings if you are using fruit or cake
- A knife to cut the fruit if needed
- A gold or purple altar cloth

First, arrange your altar to Tyche. Place the image in the center toward the rear and then group the other items around it in a pleasing manner. If you wish, add other embellishments—more candles, more images, elaborate and fancy dishes to hold the food and drink. It is appropriate to use your best.

Since you are directly petitioning a goddess rather than working a spell or performing a large ritual, you will not need to perform a quarter calling. It is not necessary to call upon deities other than the one you are petitioning. Prepare by dressing in whatever evokes worship to you, turning off electronic devices or electric lights, and putting yourself in a reflective frame of mind.

Light the candle. Say, "Tyche, Lady Luck, bringer of good fortune, please be with me and listen to my petition."

Light the incense. Say, "Tyche, Golden Lady, bringer of happiness, please accept these offerings."

Pour the wine or fruit juice into the goblet. Take a sip, and then pour a generous amount from the goblet into the libation bowl. Put the goblet back down on your altar.

If you are using fruit, divide the fruit and place half of it in the offering dish. The other half should be reserved for you and any other participants.

If you are using cake, divide the cake and place half of it in the offering dish. The other half should be reserved for you and any other participants. You may need a small kitchen knife (it does not need to be special) to neatly divide the fruit or cakes.

Place your dice or die-shaped charms on the altar. Say, "Lady Luck, please bring your golden touch to this problem in my life." Elaborate on what you want good luck with—finding a job, applying to school, adopting a child—whatever it is that you need a little luck for! Explain how being lucky will allow you to do things that are pleasing to Tyche, bearing in mind generosity and daring.

Think of this rite as an appeal to a major donor of some cause. If you were asking a wealthy and generous person in your community to give money to the animal shelter or fund a Kickstarter or help with a GoFundMe, you would tell them why their help was important; you wouldn't just say "gimme money." You would explain what positive results would come from their help.

If more than one person is doing this rite, each person should do this step in turn, explaining what they want her help for.

Then thank her. Again, if you were asking someone to help you and they agreed to, you would thank them. You, or each person, should thank her in your own words, ending with saying, "Tyche, generous benefactor, thank you for your gift of good fortune." If you have used fruit or cake, you may take a bite of the part you have reserved. (If you have multiple people, divide it so there is a bite for each.) "Thank you for this sweetness so that we share in your golden benevolence."

Now put the incense out and snuff the candle. Dispose of the libation by pouring it somewhere outdoors. You may also leave the fruit outside, but cake should be divided among participants, as it may contain things dangerous to wildlife or pets.

In the days that follow, be prepared to follow up on a lucky break that comes your way. Remember, Tyche can give you a break but she cannot follow up on it for you! You have to make the phone call, send the email, pursue the lead. You have to be daring. You have to take the chance that Lady Luck gives you.

Tyche's Correspondences

Here are some correspondences to help you honor Tyche, whether it's setting up an altar to her, planning a ritual that invokes her, or simply bringing some of her energy into your daily life.

Colors: Gold and purple. Sumptuous, gilded, decorated, lush, and rich—there is no such thing as too much.

Incense: Sandalwood, frankincense, myrrh, patchouli. Think rich, almost overwhelming scents. Frankincense and myrrh were expensive in the Hellenistic period and are therefore appropriate to Tyche.

Symbols: The most notable symbol is the cornucopia, the horn of plenty. She is often depicted holding one from which flows riches—coins, grain, grapes or fruit, or sometimes all of the above. The cornucopia brims with abundance. Decorative cornucopias are often available in autumn as Thanksgiving decorations. Fill your cornucopia with whatever symbolizes riches to you.

Festival Day: April 11, or the full moon of April

Food: Peaches, grapes, figs, or other fruits. Rich cakes are also ideal, cheesecakes or elaborate pastries, honey cakes, or baklava.

Chapter Three

Isis, Mother of the World

Isis is perhaps the best-known goddess of the Hellenistic world. Her worship spread from her native Egypt all over the Mediterranean, and in the Roman period as far north as Britain and Germany. There are many stories of Isis, for she had many faces and millions of worshipers over thousands of years. This one is told as it might have been in the first years of the Ptolemaic kingdom in Egypt, when the Persians had been expelled and the old gods of Egypt were welcomed among many in the new city of Alexandria.

Story: The Descent

You ask me to tell the story, my lady Berenike, and so I will, though I do not know if it will please you. It has no heroes like your Heracles or Perseus. But you say those are not all your stories, and not the ones women tell, so I will tell you this one as I heard it when I was a girl in Sais.

Once there was a woman named Tet who lived in a little village in the swamps of the Delta. Her two daughters were grown up and married, and though either of them would have had her come and live with them, she liked her own house and her own dog and to do things as she wished rather than being the mother-in-law in her daughter's house, always looking over the young woman's shoulder and hearing everything that passed between her and her husband. So Tet lived alone except for her hound, and she was content.

One day as she was walking by the river, her dog ran ahead and then started barking sharply, the kind of barks meant to alert. A young woman was lying on the riverbank, her face on her hands, but the movement of her back showed that she was breathing. Tet hurried to her and turned her over. Her sheath was of fine-drawn linen and her ears were pierced for jewels but she wore no ornament at all, not so much as a string of beads of painted shell. "What has happened to you?" Tet asked, raising her up as her eyelids flickered. "How did you get here? What is your name?"

The woman opened her eyes. "I don't remember," she whispered.

Tet knew something terrible must have happened. "Can you stand?" she asked. "My house isn't far." She helped the young woman to her feet, and together with her dog guided the young woman home. She laid her down on her own bed and brought water to wash the mud off her. There was dried blood on her feet but no wound. She looked at the cloth, wondering what to ask.

The woman, who had said no word since the first, looked at the cloth with anguish-filled eyes. "My husband was murdered," she said, and then she could say no more.

"Oh my dear," Tet said, and put her arms around her in a hug. "You are safe here. You must rest, and when you are stronger you can tell me what happened. And then we will appeal for justice."

"There is no justice," she said, though her arms were tight around Tet. "There is no justice, no peace, no care, and he is gone from me forever." And she wept.

In the days that followed the young woman seemed stronger. She said her name was Aset, but she refused to tell Tet who had committed the murder, nor would she give names of any who knew her. "I don't remember," she said, over and over.

Tet shook her head as she washed beans for dinner, sloshing them around in the bottom of the pot to soften them. The young woman was highborn; there was no doubt of that. She didn't know how to wash beans or sweep a floor or make a fire. Her hands were long and soft. And yet she was kind and willing, affectionate to the dog and happy to help at any task, unskilled as her help might be. But she would not consider going to the city or making any appeal for justice. "He will kill me," was all she said.

The third night she was there was the full moon. Tet woke when her dog stirred. He didn't growl, just alerted with his ears pricked forward. A gray tabby cat was mounting the front steps built into the pilings that held the house above floodwaters. The cat paused, looking straight at the dog, who put his head down on his paws. Then the cat simply walked in, keeping an eye on Tet and the dog, and headbutted Aset.

Aset lifted her head, and the cat butted her again. "Oh!" Aset said. "You found me!" She put her arms around the cat, who purred and curled up against her.

Tet refrained from asking, "Is this your cat?" because obviously it was. Where had it come from? It couldn't have come far, but she could think of no one nearby who had recently been murdered. It was a small town, like other small towns in the Delta. If a young man had been brutally murdered and his wife gone missing, everyone would have been talking of it for years!

In the coming days, Tet asked after the gossip in town each time she saw anyone, and no one spoke of a murder. No one spoke of a missing woman. It was very strange. And yet Aset was clearly frightened of someone, so Tet did not tell her story. When friends commented that she was buying food for two, she said that a friend of her daughter's had come to stay with her because she was recently widowed and no longer welcome in her in-laws house, an explanation that seemed to satisfy everyone. Before long, Aset would even come into the village with her, shy and with her eyes downcast. She did not speak of herself at all but listened with pleasure to all the stories the villagers told her. Too soon to think of horror, Tet thought, and there was something more.

There was an old man who had something wrong with his eyes. They were inflamed and he could not see to work, so he sat before his house and begged help of all who passed. Many pitied him, but none could help. Tet was trading some fish she had caught and missed the beginning of it, but she came when she heard the commotion. The man was standing up, his eyes wide. "I can see!" he shouted. "I can see! She healed me!"

Aset stood nearby with a bowl. "I did nothing," she said quietly, "except give the old man some water." She tipped the bowl up. "See? There is nothing in it but water."

"I can see!" he shouted again, and indeed his sight was restored, but no one could find any reason for it. After all, she had only given him water.

It did not escape Tet that forty days passed and Aset did not bleed. Her waist was narrow, but there was a curve beneath it that would not have been obvious on someone less slender. "Yes," Aset said, "it is true. I carry my husband's child. If his murderer knew, he would kill me in an instant, and here I have no power."

Tet put her hand over the young woman's. "Sweetheart, where do you have power? I can't help you if you don't tell me anything. Surely you have kin who are worried about you. Surely if your husband had powerful enemies he also had powerful friends."

The cat came and stood beside her, turning and turning its way into Aset's lap. "There is no one who can stand against him," Aset said. "Not now. The only one who will be able to is the Blameless Prince."

"And where is this Blameless Prince?" Tet asked.

"Here," she said, curving her hand over her belly.

The child was born on the first night of the Inundation, when the waters rose around the little house until it stood like a boat at sea above the flood. Tet caught him when he came forth, lying him on his mother's breast before she cut his cord with steel. It was a boy, of course. His high cries were stopped with the breast, his tiny hands closing against his mother's skin. The dog and the cat sat together watching approvingly.

"I love you so, my darling," his mother said while Tet wiped her brow with cool water. "You will restore justice. My sweet, my baby, my prince."

And of course he did. You know the story by now, my lady Berenike. When Set killed Osiris and Isis fled the peaceful West, she descended to us. She hid in the Delta and there she bore her son and raised him until he could avenge his father and restore Ma'at— justice, peace, and the order of the world as it is supposed to be.

Isis alone of the gods has lived as a mortal woman. She has known suffering. She has swept floors and washed beans and borne her son in pain. She has loved as mortals do, not with the timeless detachment of the gods. For this reason, we name her Mother of the World. She does not belong to one people or city but to all who struggle here. She has compassion, for she has known sorrow as we have. You are a widow, my lady Berenike. You have two children. If she speaks to you, it is because you are hers, even though you were born in a foreign land. Isis welcomes you.

Questions to Consider

Now that you have read a story about Isis, take out your journaling materials, either paper and a writing implement or an electronic means of journaling. It's time to consider your reaction to the story you just read.

- What is your immediate emotional reaction to Isis's story? How does it make you feel?

- One of Isis' aspects is cthonic, as Queen of the Underworld. What do you think of the idea that our world is the underworld, the place one descends from the beautiful West?

- How did you feel about a vulnerable goddess? What about an embodied goddess who is helpless?

- Many ancient stories include a common person who takes in a deity without knowing who they are and shows them hospitality. What did you think of Tet and how does it fit with your understanding of the Divine?

Ancient Worship: Isis

Isis has many epithets, but perhaps the most common is Mother of the World. She is portrayed many different ways, but the most common is seated with her son on her lap or at her breast. She was celebrated as a universal mother, the mother of all people no matter where they came from, and her worship welcomed everyone.

Before the Hellenistic period, Isis was exclusively an Egyptian goddess, albeit a very old one who was part of the Ennead, the nine gods who comprised the major deities of the Egyptian pantheon. Her worship in particular spread rapidly in this syncretic world. Temples of Isis have been uncovered from the British Isles to Ethiopia, from the Black Sea to Morocco. Thus, there is a great range of ancient worship practices attested to. Some written documents explain some things about it—for example, Plutarch's *Moralia* explains how the clergy of Isis he was familiar with conducted themselves, including what they wore and what food restrictions they observed, including not eating freshwater fish. However, his description is a snapshot of a particular place and time that he himself says is not definitive. There is also archaeological evidence. For example, the Temple of Isis at Pompeii is well preserved and serves as an example from a Roman town in Italy rather than from Egypt. There are other written sources, including Apuleius's novel *The Golden Ass*, written a century later and once again in a different location, and many other archaeological sites. In short, the question of how Isis was worshiped in the Hellenistic world is complex, and I encourage you to consider more than one source if you delve more deeply into the subject.

Still, there are common threads, and it is those threads we will examine further with the understanding that they only present part of a larger, complicated picture.

Meeting Isis: A Meditation

This meditation may be done in two different ways: Find a partner to read it to you and take turns doing the meditation, or simply read it in a quiet place or even record it and play it to yourself.

You will need a quiet place where you won't be disturbed for twenty minutes or so. You may play soft music if you like. If you have music you normally use while meditating, you may certainly use it. If you would like to use incense, consider one of the recommendations in the correspondences section at the end of this chapter.

This may be an intense experience. Read through the meditation before you begin and decide if it is something you want to do.

Take a deep breath to help you relax. Then take another. Now begin either reading to yourself or listening as the meditation is read to you. If you are having it read to you, close your eyes. Otherwise, read aloud slowly so that you have time to absorb the words.

You are outdoors on a trail that winds among the trees. The sound of children's shouts and laughter fills the air. You are at a zoo or perhaps a children's museum or a science park. There are signs that indicate where different things are, and there are children everywhere running delightedly from place to place, excited to see everything. Perhaps you are a child yourself. Perhaps you are a parent or grandparent. Or perhaps you are simply someone who also enjoys zoos or science parks. In any event, you are strolling along the trails, enjoying the exhibits as much as the children.

The trees are big and old, and you turn down a trail that seems to lead to a quieter area. Almost immediately, you can hear birdsong. There are no crowds here. It's simply peaceful and you walk along the trail, enjoying the beauty around you. Truly, the world is a beautiful place.

A young woman steps out from between the trees. She smiles at you. Though she's casually dressed and seems normal, there is something about her…something odd and lovely. She is the young teacher children cry on when hurt, the woman who stops her car by the road to help a lost dog, the babysitter who runs across the playground to check on a child who has fallen and skinned their knee, even if they aren't hers. You know her face. You may have seen it long ago in some barely remembered moment in early childhood, or you may know it well. You may have even worn her face, seen it in pictures of you and been startled by its piercing beauty. She is Isis. She is the Mother of the World.

Now is your chance to greet her. She takes your hands and sits down with you on a bench under the trees. Here in this peaceful place with the laughter of children in the distance, you can tell her your troubles. You can pour out the sadness in your heart to one you know will understand and listen with compassion. You can tell her your pain. She will listen. She will ask nothing in return. She will require nothing of you. She simply wants to help by listening.

As you talk with her, she nods with understanding. She makes eye contact. She holds your hands if you find that comforting. She will let you cry on her shoulder if you wish. You are safe. You are seen. You are accepted.

It may be that she asks questions, drawing you out. It may be that she simply listens in compassionate silence. In any event, she does not attempt to interpret your sorrows or tell you what to do or judge you. She simply receives them.

When at last you are finished, she puts her arms around you, holding you tight. "You are beloved," she says. "It will be alright." You feel a sense of peace in her words. "Even when it seems impossible, it will be alright," she says. You know she means it. You know she's lived it. She's been a young, pregnant woman whose husband was brutally murdered, in fear for her life, taking refuge among strangers. And yet somehow, she came through it. Somehow she relearned joy. When she says it will be alright, you know that somehow, sometime, it will be.

Rest on her. Rest on the goddess until you are ready to leave. There is no time limit. There is nothing asked of you, and you may return to her at any time.

When you are ready, stand up and let go of her if you are touching. "You can come and see me when you want," she says. "You know the way." She gestures to the path that runs between the trees, the path through a place dedicated to happiness and knowledge.

"Thank you," you say. You add your own words of thanks to the Mother of the World. It is as though you have left some part of your burden here in the clearing under the trees, some part of the heaviness you carry in your heart with her. She will keep it for you. She will hold it for you, safe and respected and protected.

You walk away, back toward the main paths, knowing that you can return anytime you wish. As you walk, the paths curve back toward your everyday world.

You open your eyes.

When you are fully back, turn off any music and put out any incense. Think for a moment about your experience. What did it feel like? How do you feel now? This may have been a very intense meditation. You may wish to ground by eating or drinking. You may want to take a shower to help return to the physical present.

What did it feel like to experience her unconditional love? Was it safe or scary? Do you feel energized or drained? If you are journaling, you may wish to write about this experience. Take the time you need to process it.

Lessons from Isis: Mother of the World

Now that we've read a story about Isis and done a meditation to meet her, let's talk a little bit about her gifts.

Compassion

As we saw in the story, Isis treasures compassion, which is more than just caring: it's putting yourself in someone's shoes, asking "how would I feel if I were them?" Very often when we give, we give what we think people should want, not what they really want. Sometimes it's small things. I give my daughter the sensible shoes I think are practical and lasting, not the impractical shoes that will make her feel beautiful. We, as a society, give WIC program members the food we think they ought to have, regardless of whether it is the food they want or need. Compassion requires us to imagine how we would like to be in the other person's situation.

Isis also does not give for the sake of credit, but purely for the sake of easing pain. As we see in the story, she heals the old man's eyes and does not ask anything of him in return. She doesn't ask that he profess a certain creed. She doesn't ask whether he's a good enough person to deserve healing. She doesn't even take credit for the act. She simply heals him because he needs it. And yet one of the first things I learned working for nonprofits is that donors expect to be lavishly praised for giving. They expect perks and awards, constant recognition, and thanks. The more they give, · the more fulsome praise they expect, which was also the case in the Hellenistic world. For example, after Ptolemy I's navy rescued the city of Rhodes from a rival army, the city voted him the title of Savior, which he used for the rest of his life. Ptolemy the Savior— that's a big reward! It's true that people will give more when they receive praise, but that is not how Isis gives. She gives her compassionate gifts simply because people need them, without expectation of reward.

If you would have Isis's favor, try this: give anonymously. Help simply because you can. Don't put requirements on your compassion, e.g., "I will only help you eat if you eat the right food." Put yourself in their shoes.

Resilience

Isis's story is full of suffering: her husband is murdered, she flees, she searches for his body, weeping. She finds it and puts the pieces together so that he can be whole in the afterlife. She animates him so that she may conceive a child. She hides in the swamps in exile to bear her child among strangers and raises him alone. She is a single mother, the wife of a murdered man. And yet, she is strong. She is brave. She is loving. She spreads compassion and joy wherever she goes. Stories tell us that she invented beer "for men's delight." She sings, she dances, she plays the sistrum. Isis is made stronger by her suffering. She is made more aware of the preciousness of life, of the beauty of the people around her. She loves because she understands. She too has been through things.

If we are lucky, we know someone who embodies this gift of Isis, someone whose own pain has made them into a refuge for others. Isis is the perfect goddess to ask for resilience. She has been there, deep in pain and loss, and she offers a path to the other side. She does not strike out in anger but reaches out in love. She does not destroy. She rebuilds. She turns toward life, not away. She does not let her suffering define her or rob her life of joy or the future that she and her son may build together.

Mercy

The Mother of the World loves all her children, even the ones who misbehave. You don't have to be good to be worthy of her love. You simply have to exist. However, that doesn't mean that Isis has no boundaries. A loving parent doesn't simply let children do whatever they want if it means they harm themselves or others. A loving parent tries to guide their children to make good choices and prevents them from doing things that will hurt others. If they do hurt others, their parents will still love them but won't support their actions. Love, compassion, and mercy do not require saying that harmful behavior is okay. If you are a person with regrets, it is supremely comforting to know that bad decisions don't mean that you are forever lost. She may not approve, but she understands and extends her mercy to everyone who comes to her with a remorseful heart.

What about the people who feel no remorse? What about those who keep on justifying hurting others? Isis does not approve, but she also doesn't hate. As a mother with a wayward teen does, she hopes that the person will grow up and change. When they do, she will be waiting with her mercy, ready to welcome them home.

Justice

Isis is also the dispenser of justice. She rules beside her husband in the West, in the afterlife, and sees the souls of the dead brought before them for judgment. However, she also dispenses justice in the world. But beware if you ask for her justice because she does not like revenge! Nor does she approve of justice that harms the innocent incidentally. She prefers restitution to retribution.

Because she is Mother of the World and therefore all peoples are equal in her eyes, Isis specifically does not like punishments that fall indiscriminately on everyone in a group. She is not the "smite all our enemies" kind of goddess. Justice is a thin-bladed knife whose purpose is to restore to the victim what has been taken from them, not a hatchet that destroys those who hurt you. Since restoration is her goal, her justice may not take the form you imagine. After all, her goal is healing and restoration. This may ultimately have little to do with the person who wronged them.

As we see in the story, her husband cannot be restored to his throne as a living man. The murder cannot be erased. Justice can only come in the next generation, when her son will claim the throne and restore balance, those last two words being the most important. Her son will bring his father's murderer to justice but the goal isn't to punish—it is to return the world to a better state for everyone who lives in it. Killing her husband's murderer will not bring him back—that is impossible, even for a goddess. Bringing the murderer to justice will instead allow society to heal from his misdeeds and rule as the evil king. Isis will be restored to the throne but not as the king's wife. She will be his mother: older and wiser, standing beside the throne as she is portrayed in so many reliefs.

A Rite to Honor Isis

This is a rite to honor Isis and to bring her love into your life. It is designed for one person alone but can be adapted if you wish to do it with others.

You Will Need

- An image of Isis: You may have a statuette or the like as they are commonly available, or you may make or draw your own. You may also simply print out an image of Isis.
- A heart: It may be of any material you like—ceramic, stone, metal, even a cut-out paper heart. Note that if you have more than one person, you will need one each. If you prefer, you may use a heart-shaped charm that can be worn
- A red candle of any size you wish
- Incense and a burner, preferably lotus or kyphi
- A small pitcher of wine or fruit juice
- A goblet or cup
- A libation bowl

Optional Extras

- A red altar cloth
- Red paper and writing utensils (if you have a larger group)
- Evocative music and a way to play it

First, arrange your altar to Isis: place the image in the center back, and then group the other items pleasingly around it. You may add other embellishments if you wish—more candles, more images, elaborate and fancy dishes to hold the food and drink. It is appropriate to use your best.

Since you are directly petitioning a goddess rather than working a spell or performing a large ritual, you will not need to perform a quarter calling. It is not necessary to call upon deities other than the one you are petitioning.

Prepare by dressing in whatever evokes worship to you, turning off electronic devices or electric lights, and putting yourself in a reflective frame of mind. If you are playing music, you may start the music now.

Light the candle and then the incense if you are using it. Take a moment to center yourself. Say, "Gracious Lady, Mother of the World, please attend my petition. You who have known both love and loss reach out with compassion to all of your children. Please hear what is upon my heart."

Then tell her in your own words what troubles you. Try not to be full of anger and blame, though sorrow is fine. For example, phrase it as, "I am sad because a relationship has ended that was very important to me. I am both sorrowful and worried that I will never be loved as I need to be," rather than, "My former lover was a terrible person and I don't think I will find someone better." She will understand your meaning either way, but try to focus on how you feel rather than on the other person or their actions. You are asking her to console you, whatever your sorrow, as well as to bring love into your life, not to punish someone else.

Your words do not have to be relationship focused. For example, "Mother of the World, I am sorrowful that I will bear no more children. Please help me open my heart to an adoptive or foster child so that our lives will be filled with love instead of sadness." Another example: "Mother of the World, I have lost someone dear to me. I have mourned and now am ready to entertain the idea of loving someone again. Please help me learn joy again." Isis is ready to console you. Just be sure that you are keeping the focus of your petition on you, not on others. She will not respond well to "Make my ex come back to me."

If you and more than one person are doing this rite together, give each person a chance to speak in turn. If you have a larger group and people are not comfortable sharing their feelings with everyone, you can have each person write a letter to Isis on the red paper, taking their time to make their petition thoughtfully. Then they can fold their letter and place it on the altar. This is actually a very old way of making a request of Isis! Petitions to the goddess have been found that are thousands of years old. Like yours, they ask for her help with problems of the heart.

When you have made your request, pour the wine or fruit juice into the cup. Pour a libation to her into the libation bowl. Say, "Gracious Lady, thank you for listening. Let us share this, as I have shared my sorrows and wishes with you." Then drink the portion that remains in the cup, mindful that you are sharing with Isis.

Take the heart that you have prepared, whatever material it is made of. Put your fingertips on it. Say, "Mother of the World, let my heart be filled." Close your eyes. Imagine her love pouring into the heart, filling it up and charging it until the heart is simply brimming with it. Feel the heart under your fingers. Feel it as a tangible symbol of her love. When you are ready, lift the heart and hold it to your own. Feel the synchronicity between them. Let this repository of love touch you, uplift you, and begin to fill your own heart.

When you are ready, step back, open your eyes, and thank her in your own words. If there is more than one person doing the rite, each person should have a turn to do this.

Keep the heart. Put it somewhere you will see it every day. On your altar is fine if you have a permanent one, or on a bedside table or a windowsill or desk. If your heart is a charm that can be worn, wear it often, especially when you feel the need of love in your life.

Say, "Gracious Isis, thank you for your attention and your comfort. As you loved fearlessly and deeply, let me also love." Blow out the candle. Put out the incense. Pour the libation outside onto the ground. Be thankful for her presence in your life.

In the days to come, try to embody Isis's compassion and mercy in your own actions. Be mindful that resilience comes from love and from taking chances to reach out to others even when one is wounded oneself. Learn from her blessings.

Isis's Correspondences

Here are some correspondences to help you honor Isis, whether it's setting up an altar to her, planning a ritual that invokes her, or simply bringing some of her energy into your daily life.

Colors: Blue, red, gold

Incense: Lotus, jasmine, or kyphi

Symbols: Ankh, lotus flower, cobra, sistrum, throne, and many others, depending on her specific role

Festival Day: July 23

Food: Bread, dates, honey, beer.[10] It is especially appropriate to offer beer rather than wine to Isis as one of her stories is

---

10. DeTraci Regula, *The Mysteries of Isis* (St. Paul MN: Llewellyn Publications, 1996), 156–158.

the how Isis invented beer and gave it to people as a way of preserving grain. However, in the Hellenistic period she was often offered wine as most gods were, so if you prefer wine that is fine. Isis has many other correspondences as well. She was worshiped so widely for so long, and with so many different attributes celebrated, that she amassed a huge body of different symbols and stories.

These are a few correspondences to begin with. If you are curious, there are any number of fine modern books dedicated to the worship of Isis.[11]

11. Sophia, *The Ultimate Guide to Goddess Empowerment* (Kansas City, KS: Andrews McMeel Publishing, 2003), 120–123.

Chapter Four

Athena, Companion of Heroes

Athena is one of the best known of the Greek gods. She is the goddess of wisdom and strategy, invoked as the protector of democracy. Her worship was widespread in the Hellenistic world. Not only was she the patron of the city of Athens, where the Parthenon, her remarkable temple, still stands today, but she was also worshiped at many temples from the Silk Road of central Asia to Spain. Her worship therefore encompassed many different things at different times. She had a variety of names, from Athena Parthenos ("Virgin, Ever Pure") to Athena Strategos ("Wise in War"). It is in that last capacity that she is the companion of heroes, the goddess at their back who inspires them to think creatively and win through smarts. The strong-man heroes who swing a big club and knock everyone off their feet are not for her! She preferred heroes like clever Odysseus, who led the Greeks to victory in the Trojan War by means of a ruse, constructing a wooden horse which he and several other men hid in and were taken into the city, sneaking out at night to open the gates. Athena likes strategy. It's not about how many enemies you kill or how big your muscles are but how smart you are.

In historic times leaders were likened to Odysseus because of their cleverness. One such was Themistocles, whose patron goddess was Athena. Here is a story which in the Hellenistic world you would have heard as history, the story of true events that happened only a hundred and fifty years earlier.

Story: Wily Themistocles

They say the gods take no hand in the affairs of people today, but that's not true. Never was the hand of a goddess clearer than for Themistocles of Athens. Cynics say he was just a good politician, but isn't politics strategy? I put it to you that elections are as much strategy as war, and Themistocles won on that field as much as the other. No, he didn't win all the time. No one does, whether by ballot or on a ship facing the fleet of the enemy. But he won by Athena's grace when it mattered, and we and all Greece should be thankful for it.

It was in the great war against Persia when the Emperor Xerxes decided that all the cities of Greece would pay tribute to him as though we were mere client states. Some gave him earth and fire, such as a pot of dirt from their land and a pot of burning coals but many refused, and chief among those was Athens. Athens had no king but a democracy under the patronage of the goddess of the city, Athena Parthenos, and they had fought the Persians before. It was a long and bloody war. You know the story of the three hundred Spartans who held the pass at Thermopylae until all of them were killed. Well, this is what happened after that. The Persians marched on toward Athens.

Now Themistocles was the elected leader at that time, and he knew that the Athenians could not defeat the Persians on land. The Persian army was enormous and had just defeated the Spartans, who had the finest army in Greece. He knew that Athens's strength lay in her navy, not her army. He believed it was the best navy in the world, and it probably was. In the last ten years Themistocles himself had gotten Athens to vote money to build a hundred new ships, and each ship had rowers who were free men, citizens who did their service to the city thus, and they were drilled and ready. There were archers too—Cretans—who were allies of Athens and served on the ships. And most of all, there were sailors aplenty who knew their business because Athens made her fortune from the sea. Themistocles himself had served at sea.

He wasn't a young and handsome hero. He was fifty, bearded and stocky. His father had been a citizen, but his mother was an immigrant from Caria in Asia Minor. He'd grown up in the sprawling wooden low city outside the walls where the poor lived. But that was Athens in that day. Even a man of such modest birth could find favor with Athena! You see, for whatever reason the goddess had marked him. He was devoted to her and to her city. And was he not the kind of man she always favored, clever and driven, ideals tempered by bitter practicality?

So when Themistocles had word that the Persians marched on Athens from Thermopylae, he knew the city could not stand. The people would be slaughtered and the survivors taken away to Asia Minor as slaves. Therefore he ordered an evacuation. There was an island just a little off the coast, Salamis, with a narrow strait between it and the mainland. The island was rocky and easily defended, and more importantly the only way to take it would be by landing an invasion force by sea. If the people of Athens went there, the fleet could defend them. You can imagine the debate in the Assembly! Desert the city, abandon homes and businesses, even the temple of Athena herself, the Parthenon! And yet Themistocles argued. "Houses and shops can be rebuilt. Even Athena's own house can be rebuilt! But Athens is her people, not her buildings! If we die in defense of them and our children are carried away to toil in the Persian Emperor's far-off lands, what is Athens then?"

At last, in fear and rage, the evacuation began. Every ship was pressed into service to ferry people to the island. By the time the Persian vanguard was sighted, the people were gone except for those who would not leave the temples on the Acropolis. The Persians marched in. The Acropolis fell. From the island, people watched the smoke going up to the sky, Athena's own temple burning, its gilded roof crashing in. They wept. They prayed. They cursed Themistocles. Surely he should have saved the city!

Themistocles watched as well from a high point of the wall. He could see the haze of burning, the low smolder of the fires dying down. He thought of the city he had loved all his life, from the crowded lower town to the Parthenon. Perhaps he saw Athena herself leaving the ruins of her temple to light beside him on the wall in the form of her sacred owl, wisdom that flies by night, hunting on silent, unseen wings. Her hand was on his shoulder.

He leaned upon the parapet and thought of what he knew of the Persian Emperor Xerxes: He was not a patient man. He could have starved the Spartans out at Thermopylae rather than attack them and lose so many men in the assault, but instead he was determined to win. Now, Themistocles thought, Xerxes could afford to wait. He held the mainland. Eventually the people who had taken refuge on the island would run out of food if the Persian fleet blockaded them. Themistocles smiled. To blockade the island, Xerxes would have to bring the Persian fleet in close. He would have to keep Salamis from being supplied by sea. And to do that, he would have to fight the Athenian navy.

Yes, you see the plan already, don't you? Themistocles would force the Persians to fight how he wanted. But the Persian navy was no easy target. It was larger than the Athenian, since Xerxes had all of the ports of the Eastern Mediterranean to draw ships from. However, all of these people spoke different languages. Their captains had not fought together and they answered to different lords. The queen of Halicarnassus, Artemisia, had brought her levy, but her proud sailors had never fought with the others before. Though Xerxes's admiral, Mardunaya, was a good commander, he had never led many of these men until now and he did not know these waters as Themistocles did. Themistocles thought he could win if he were clever and bold.

Meanwhile, Athens's allies were getting worried. They could see Athens burning. Would their cities be next? What was the advantage of staying and fighting a losing battle? That evening there was a council of war. Athena must have stood beside Themistocles, because he convinced the allies to stay and fight despite all their reservations. He told them his clever plan and enough believed him.

After the meeting ended, Themistocles went to where his family was staying with the other refugees and he found his children's tutor. The tutor agreed that he would take a rowboat and go over to the Persians saying that he had information. He would tell them that some of the allies had decided to leave the next day and that Themistocles was willing to betray Athens for money and safe passage for his family. If the Persians were interested, he would take the message back to Themistocles and be the go-between. Yes, what a brave man he was! If the Persians had not believed him, he would have been killed! But fortunately for him and for Athens, Athena loves a canny liar; they believed him. After all, it was what they wanted to hear. The allies were leaving at daybreak, and Themistocles could be bought. The tutor rowed back with some earnest money and the beginning of deal.

It was a ruse, of course. Now Themistocles had set a trap. In the dark, the Persian fleet began closing in around the island to keep the allies from running away. What Themistocles knew but they did not was that the water was very shallow. It meant that the smaller Greek ships had an advantage because the Persian ships would have to be very careful not to run aground and get stuck. And because it was such a tight space, they could not really use their numbers very well. Most of their fleet would be out of range with their archers too far away to hit anything.

As soon as dawn came, Themistocles attacked. A trumpet sounded and then the men at the oars began to sing. It was their victory song, and they sang as they rowed straight toward the Persian fleet. Themistocles shouted, "Sons of Hellenes, forward to freedom!" One Athenian ship darted forward, ramming a Phoenician ship of the line, and then the fleets closed.

Now you will see how clever Themistocles had been! One on one, the Greek seamanship was better. In the shallow water, they could ram and board the Persian ships. When a ship sank or they were knocked overboard, the Greeks knew how to swim and the Persians did not. In shallow water near the island, the Greeks simply swam ashore. Also, the Persians were tired from waiting at their posts all night while the Greeks were fresh. The battle raged for hours, one combat after another. The Greeks did not go after their prizes into deep water but instead waited for the enemy to come to them where they had the advantage, relying on discipline and training as well as courage.

Slowly, the tide began to turn. Xerxes watched in disbelief as one after another, his ships were sunk, captured by the Athenians, or ran aground on the rocks around the island. By the time the day ended, the Persian fleet was in splinters and running away. Themistocles had won against all odds.

What happened then? They went home, of course. The ships ferried the people back across the strait and they rebuilt their city. They cleaned the temple and repaired the statue of the goddess. They built houses and markets anew. And they gave thanks to Athena, who had put her hand on Themistocles as she had the heroes of old and showed him how to win through strategy.

Questions to Consider

- What is your immediate emotional reaction to Themistocles' story? Why do you feel that way?
- What kind of hero is Themistocles? Why do you think Athena favors him?
- How does Athena's favor compare with that of the other goddesses we have explored? How is it the same and how is it different?
- How does this story fit with your understanding of Athena? Is she a goddess you would be comfortable invoking and why or why not?

Ancient Worship: Athena

Athena loves clever tricksters, smart heroes who win with a great plan rather than by bashing everything in their way. And she is more than a goddess of battle—she is also the champion of democracy.

Champion of Democracy

The story of the Battle of Salamis is true and comes to us from a number of historical sources. One of them, the poet Aeschylus, was an eyewitness.[12] He was too old to be in the crew of a galley but was one of the older men who waited on Salamis as a last-ditch defense in case the Persians broke through. He tells us:

> The whole disaster was set in train … by some avenging power. … A Greek came from the Athenian fleet and this is what he told Xerxes, "When night's dark mantle falls, the Greeks will wait no longer but spring to their rowing benches and scatter, saving their lives by stealing away." Xerxes listened to this, not sensing Greek deception, or the gods' displeasure with him, and he gave these orders to his admirals. All night long the commanders kept their ships on station and the whole fleet at their oars, but then the night was almost over and the Greeks had made no attempt to steal away.[13]

Athena, of course, is the "avenging power," the goddess whose temple has been burned by the invading Persians. It is she who is presented standing with Themistocles as she did with Odysseus in the Iliad, her hand on his shoulder, inspiring him to cleverly entrap her foes. It is clear historically that Themistocles did defeat the Per-

12. William Shepherd, *Salamis 480 BC: The Naval Campaign that Saved Greece* (Oxford, UK: Osprey Publishing, 2010), 70–71.

13. Aeschylus, *The Persians*, trans. Robert Potter (London: Routledge & Sons, 1932), 355–385.

sians with his clever strategy.[14] One of the images of Athena from Athens in this period is an oil jar (now on display in the Metropolitan Museum) showing Athena wearing her helmet and holding a spear as she stands upon a victorious ship.[15]

Yet Athena is more than an avenger. Why is it that she favors the Athenians in the first place? It is her role as Protector of Democracy. Athens was one of the first states to have a government elected by male citizens in a world where almost every country was a monarchy. Democracy was an experiment. It might have been a short one. Only a few generations before Themistocles, Athens had overthrown an oligarchy to establish an elected government. If Athens had fallen to Persia, no doubt it would have either been under a governor or had an oligarch sympathetic to the Persians installed as ruler. The experiment with electing leaders would have been over.

Athenian democracy has inspired democratic governments around the world for more than two thousand years. It has shown that it is possible to have citizens elect their leaders, and therefore it looms larger culturally than it ever did politically. In this time, no less than in Themistocles' time, democracy is under attack. Athena is still terribly relevant as the champion of democracy.

Goddess of Strategy and Planning

One of Athena's other historical roles is as the goddess of strategy and planning. While Ares and others were the gods of war in the Hellenistic world, Athena was specifically seen as ruling over tactics

---

14. Barry Strauss, *The Battle of Salamis* (New York: Simon & Schuster, 2004), 159–161.
15. Jar attributed to the Brygos Painter, Metropolitan Museum, New York: https://www.metmuseum.org/art/collection/search/251932.

and strategy rather than physical combat. In the widely known story of the Trojan War, she helped the hero Odysseus figure out how to break the stalemate by a clever ruse. This story was widely told as an illustration that sometimes when brawn will not suffice, brains will make the difference.

But of course, strategy and planning are not just important in war—they're important in most endeavors. Constructing a road or a building requires elaborate planning. Creating a school curriculum, arranging a clinic, running a summer camp, maintaining a platform for web sales, planning the menu for a restaurant—all of these activities in the working world require planning and strategy. Athena's role encompasses all of these things. She helps us create good plans, because even good work is pointless if it is not in service to a good plan. Thus, Athena is relevant across many fields.

Meeting Athena: A Meditation

This meditation may be done in two different ways: Find a partner to read it to you and take turns doing the meditation, or simply read it in a quiet place or even record it and play it to yourself.

You will need a quiet place where you won't be disturbed for twenty minutes or so. You may play soft music if you like. If you have music you normally use while meditating, you may certainly use it. If you would like to use incense, consider one of the recommendations in the list of correspondences at the end of this chapter.

Take a deep breath to help you relax. Then take another. Now begin either reading to yourself or having the meditation read to you. If you are having it read to you, close your eyes. Otherwise, read aloud slowly so that you have time to absorb the words. This may be an intense experience, so read through the meditation before you begin and decide if it is something you want to do.

You are standing on the balcony of a building looking out across a great city. It's nighttime and the stars in the sky above your head are echoed in the million lights of the city. The city spreads beneath you like looking into a star-studded pool. Maybe it's a city you know well. Maybe it's somewhere you've imagined going. Or maybe you have no idea what this place is, only that it's beautiful and home to millions of people. Below, the streets are busy with life. There are cars, restaurants, theaters, people strolling along in the pleasant cool. The city is full of stories. Each and every life is precious, unique as a point of light in the heavens. You look down on them from a high place.

You see a movement out of the corner of your eye. An owl lands not far from you, silent except for the click of her claws on the metal rail. She fluffs out her feathers and then suddenly shifts, taking the form of a woman instead of an owl. She wears white, a silver helm upon her head, and her eyes when she looks at you are gray as steel. You know this is Athena, and you bow in reverence.

"You have come to see me," she says. "Why?" Her voice is curious, not challenging. She's not angry, just interested. She wants to know.

You tell her. You explain in your own words why you have sought her, why you wanted to meet her. Maybe it's devotion or need. Maybe it's simply curiosity. She is merely interested in your motives.

When you finish, she looks at you appraisingly. "What did you hope to learn from this?"

It's a good question. What did you hope to learn? Tell her. Maybe it's that you wanted to learn something that would help you with a problem. Maybe it's to learn more about her. Or maybe it's something entirely different. Tell Athena what you wanted to learn from this encounter.

She nods slowly. "So why do you want to know that?" *That's a harder question. You have to think about it before you speak. Is it that you want to know something that will help you reach a goal? Or that you want insight on a problem? Do you think her wisdom and strategy will help you achieve something? Or are you simply hungry for knowledge? The latter is what will endear you the most to her, but all of these are good reasons.*

Athena listens. "You will find the answers to your questions," *she says.* "It may be easier than you expect." *She smiles a thin, knowing smile.* "Remember, knowing what you want to know is half the solution. You can go far on asking the right questions." *Her smile lengthens.* "Think about it."

"I will," *you promise.*

She looks over the rail at the city twinkling in the dark. "A million people," *she says,* "and each one part of the whole. Look for the pattern and you will understand the brightness. There is wonder in nature. There is also wonder in the makings of humans and in the patterns they make to care for one another. It is no less beautiful than untouched forests or wild seas." *Athena glances at you again.* "Think about it," *she directs.* "And know that you can reach me here if you want to."

Before you have the chance to say something more or even draw a breath, she transforms again, the owl launching herself

from the railing, gliding on silent wings over the bright city below.
You watch in awe. She looks down upon her people, and you
watch her until she is out of sight.

Then you return to the present, slowly, peacefully. You open
your eyes.

Turn off recorded music if you are using any. Put out candles
and incense. Say, "Thank you, Athena, Bright One, for speaking
with me." Know that you can indeed return to the balcony above
the city whenever you wish to speak with her again.

Think for a moment about your experience. What did it feel
like? How do you feel now? This may have been a very intense
meditation. You may wish to ground by eating or drinking and
also take a shower to help return to the physical present.

What did it feel like to talk to Athena. Was it safe or scary? Do
you feel energized or drained? If you are journaling, you may wish
to write about this experience. Take the time you need to process it.

Lessons from Athena: Companion of Heroes

Now that we've read a story about Athena and done a meditation
to meet her, let's talk a little bit about her gifts. Athena was known
as "bright-eyed," which we may interpret as a description of her
appearance but is better translated as "keen-sighted." Athena sees
through problems to their core and thus has the insight to solve
them. All of us, at various times in our lives and our endeavors,
need her insight to help us understand how to best tackle some
situation. Here are some ways in which Athena brings clarity to
things.

Thinking Things Through

One of her great gifts is to think things through. Very often when we're faced with a problem, our instinct is to react. Many times, however, our first impulse may not be the best answer. We need to stop and think. We need to carefully consider our next move rather than simply react. Being strategic will serve us better in the long run.

For example, let's say you're buying a car. Many people who are trying to sell you a car will try to stampede you into a deal. They'll say things like, "One day only," "I've got another buyer who's very interested," "You don't need your mechanic to look at it. It's certified," "Our financing is the best rate you'll get," and so on. How many of those things are true? A wise car buyer takes all of these with a grain of salt. Maybe it's a great deal, maybe it isn't. But a smart shopper realizes that trying to get you to decide without thinking the deal through is suspect. The only way you'll know if it's the best rate is to compare. The only way you'll know if the car is sound is to get someone other than the seller to look at it. It's better to take a little more time and get more information than it is to buy a car that you'll regret.

Athena urges us to caution. Like Themistocles, we are often faced with thorny situations that don't have easy answers. Success depends on many complex variables. We need to consider carefully, get information, and make an informed decision rather than leaping to do the first thing that comes to mind. Most of the time it's better to slow down and make a good decision rather than a fast one.

Letting Go of Presuppositions

Another thing Athena helps with is letting go of our presuppositions. We often build invisible walls around our thoughts. It can't be this or that because those are impossible or at least unthinkable. Of course, sometimes we're wrong. We assume that a certain candidate can't win or that a person will respond in a certain way to what we do or that other people have the same motivations that we do. And we're wrong. Other people act in ways that seem unpredictable not because they truly are, but because our presuppositions prevented us from seeing their real motivations.

For example, if we have the presupposition that all our employees want to make as much money as possible, we are ignoring that some of them might prefer flexible schedules to more money. Some might prefer more interesting assignments, even if that came with the same salary. Some might value professional development over cash. Some might consider their ethical boundaries more important than making more money. If we hold to the presupposition that what others want is money, we may be missing what would actually motivate our employees. The way to find out is to ask. Again, we need to slow down, think things through, and gather more data.

Themistocles knew what the Persian fleet was doing because he'd gathered information; he wasn't guessing. He knew their ships would be trapped in shallow water because he knew how deep it needed to be for them to sail and he knew how deep the water was around the island. He had the relevant data points. He didn't simply suppose. Part of strategy, part of Athena's gift, is to let go of presuppositions and analyze the current situation accurately.

Following Your Insight

Inspiration is an idea that comes out of the blue. Insight is an idea that comes from putting together relevant information. In the story, Themistocles fooled the Persians with a ruse by sending his children's' tutor to them with a fake deal. This was absolutely clever and insightful, but it was based on the information he'd gathered. Once he had all the pieces, he followed them where they led. It's the last step in formulating strategy. Get the information. Put aside your presuppositions. And then follow your insight to the conclusion. He knew they believed that the allies would run. He knew they thought the Athenians would be demoralized by the burning of the city. He knew that Xerxes wasn't willing to be patient. When Themistocles put those pieces together, he saw how vulnerable they were and offered a deal that was too good to be true.

Often, this is the point where we second-guess ourselves. It's too crazy. It's too out there. It's too risky. But if you've done the previous two steps, the risk is calculated. Themistocles balanced the risk of battle against the risk of staying on the island with limited food and a city's worth of refugees. He got the information he needed and then followed his insight even though the plan seemed dangerous.

Now that we have met Athena in a meditation and read a story about her as the Companion of Heroes, here is a ritual to ask her to help us with a problem in our own lives that needs strategy and planning.

A Rite to Honor Athena

This rite to honor Athena involves asking her to help you with something you need to make a plan or strategy to accomplish. It may be related to your work or a personal goal that is complex to achieve. For example, if your goal is to buy a house, there are many moving parts—polishing your credit rating, finding a reputable realtor to work with, deciding on a price range and area, being preapproved for a mortgage, and so on. You will need planning and strategic thinking to be successful. If your goal is to go back to school, you will need to find the right school, look into financial aid, scholarships, or assistantships, and anticipate the application process—a long, daunting task for which you will need a strategy. Think about what you are working on in your life that requires complicated planning. It can be anything as long as it is not something harmful to someone else.

This rite is designed for one person alone but can be adapted if you wish to do it with others. If you are doing this with multiple people, each one will need a symbol of Athena's help—a charm, statuette, or piece of artwork that illustrates an owl.

You Will Need

- An image of Athena—You may have a statue or the like as they are commonly available, or you may make or draw your own. You may use an image of an owl instead if you prefer.
- A blue or gray candle in any size you like
- Incense and a burner, preferably pine, oak, or cedar
- A small pitcher of wine or fruit juice
- A goblet or cup
- A libation bowl
- Paper and a writing implement

Optional Extras

- A blue or gray altar cloth that will fit the altar you are using
- Evocative music and a way to play it
- Images or statuettes of owls

First, arrange your altar to Athena. Place the image in the center back and then group the other items pleasingly around it. You may add other embellishments if you wish—more candles or images of owls or feathers. If you wish, you may dress in white or gray for the rite. Make sure that you have the paper and writing implement where you can reach them.

Since you are directly petitioning a goddess rather than working a spell or performing a large ritual, you will not need to perform a quarter calling. It is not necessary to call upon deities other than the one you are petitioning.

Prepare by turning off electronic devices or electric lights and putting yourself in a reflective frame of mind. If you are playing music, you may start the music now.

Light the candle and then the incense if you are using it. Pour wine or fruit juice into the goblet or cup. Say, "Athena, Companion of Heroes, I (we) ask that you attend." Pour a libation in the bowl. Say, "Athena, Goddess of Strategy, please accept my offering as you did the offerings of old, that it may be to your honor." Take a sip from the cup. Then put the cup on the altar.

Now that you have Athena's attention, explain in your own words what it is you want her help with. Take as much time as you need, explaining what it is that you are trying to do, why it is complicated, and what you would like her help with. For example,

"I would like your help with qualifying for a mortgage. There are so many different deals with so many different banks and organizations, and I would like your help in deciding which one is best for me and qualifying for it." Or, "I am trying to get into college, and I need help with the complicated applications and with deciding which ones to apply to." If you are doing this rite with other people, each person can take a turn to explain what it is they need help with.

Once you have asked for her help, give her the opportunity to answer her. With the paper and writing implement and while sitting in her silence, write or sketch on the page whatever comes to mind in terms of your plan. It may be a flow chart; it may be a list of things you need to look into; it may be a drawing of your goal. Take some time in silence without distraction to allow Athena to clarify your process. It doesn't have to be perfect. Remember, as Voltaire said, "Perfect is the enemy of good."[16] Trying to make things perfect often prevents us from making things good. Don't get hung up on perfection—these are simply notes for you. Hopefully what you create will help you work toward your goal, but it does not need to be polished.

When you have taken some time to do this and everyone is ready to move on (if you are doing this with others), put down your paper and writing implements. Stand in front of the altar and address Athena. Say, "Athena, Companion of Heroes, goddess of strategy, thank you for your help with my goal. I honor you and thank you."

---

16. Susan Ratcliffe, *Concise Oxford Dictionary of Quotations*, (Oxford, UK: Oxford Publishing, 2011), 389.

Blow out the candles, put out the incense if you are using it, and empty the libation bowl outside if possible. If there is wine left in the cup, drink it or share it but do not pour it out.

Take some time to think about this rite over the next few days. You may find that your thinking about the process has become "unstuck." You may find that you have greater clarity about what your goal is. If you wish to repeat the rite, you may. Be thankful for Athena's hand on your shoulder.

Athena's Correspondences

Here are some correspondences to help you honor Athena, whether it's setting up an altar to her, planning a ritual that invokes her, or simply bringing some of her energy into your daily life.

Colors: Blue, white, gray

Incense: Pine, oak, palmarosa, cedar

Symbols: Owl, helm, galley (oared ship), shield and spear

Festival Day: August 1

Food: Olives

Chapter Five

Atargatis, Mermaid of the Great River

Atargatis is little known today but in the Hellenistic period her worship was widespread. She was one of the patron goddesses of the Seleucid Empire, a kingdom that at its height stretched from modern Turkey through Syria, Iraq, Iran, and northward into Turkmenistan. Seleucid influence was even more widespread—images of Atargatis have been found as far west as France. As Dea Sura (a contraction of *Dea Syria*, "the goddess from Syria") she was popular during the Roman period throughout the empire. However, compared to goddesses like Isis, she is comparatively unknown today, a direct result of the limited amount of material available that survives from classical times.[17] Quite simply, less is

17. Per Bilde, "Atargatis/Dea Syria: Hellenization of Her Cult" in *Religion and Religious Practice in the Seleucid Kingdom*, volume 1 (Oxford, UK: Aarhus University Press, 1996), 153–155.

known about her from writings. Today, archaeology is beginning to fill in some of the gaps, but what we know about her mostly comes from stories and legends in which she is not the main actor.

This story of Atargatis and Sammuramat is based on a version told by Diodorus Siculus, a Hellenistic author of the first century BCE, who had heard the stories told across the Mediterranean in his time.[18] However, whether Diodorus knew it or not, Sammuramat is based on a real person, a queen in the Neo-Assyrian empire about eight hundred years before his time. She was as distant in time from Diodorus as Eleanor of Aquitaine is from us.[19] Yet then as now, stories of queens of long ago inspired, entertained, and sparked new stories. Read on for yet a new version of the story!

Story: Thunder of Heaven

Once long ago, there was a young fisherman named Hadad. He lived with his mother in a house on stilts in the reeds of the marshes outside the great city of Babylon, and he fished in the great river that we call the Euphrates. He had a little boat, just big enough for one man and his catch. Hadad was a very handsome young man, and he was also clever and hardworking. He knew the paths of the river—the main channels and all the backwaters among the swampy islands where fish spawned. He often left home just before evening fell because he knew that many of the fish fed at sunset and at night, when it was clear and cooler and the mosquitoes buzzed over the water—perfect for fish to snap up.

One night he was fishing and it was growing late. The moon had risen and made a path of light across the broad waters. He

18. Diodorus Siculus, *The Library of History Book II,* trans. C. Bedford Welles (Cambridge, MA: Harvard University Press, 1963), 161–162.
19. Georges Roux, *Ancient Iraq* (London: Penguin Books, 1992), 300–303.

heard a splash. Hadad turned because he thought it was a big fish that he could perhaps get with his net. Bobbing in the water of the main channel was a woman! Her head and shoulders were above water, long dark hair floating and flowing around her, and her eyes were the dark gray of banked storm clouds. She looked at him and smiled.

Hadad's first thought was that somehow a young woman had fallen in the river and he needed to rescue her, and his second was that this was no ordinary young woman. "Who are you?" he asked.

She smiled and then dove beneath the water with sinuous grace. She came up next to the boat and rested her arms on the side of it, her beautiful bare breasts just above the water. "You're a smart one," she said. "That's the right question."

"Will you answer it?" he said, wetting his lips. Hadad knew the stories.

Her smile grew. "My name is Atargatis, and you are Hadad. I've seen you before many times. You fish this stretch of river. You work in the hot sun hauling nets in. And in the moonlight." She moved again, and there was a *plish* sound as her tail broke the surface, green and silver scales glinting. She was half woman and half fish, you see, with a woman's upper body and a strong tail with two flukes, like a dolphin.

"You're a river spirit."

"*The* river spirit," she said with a toss of her hair. "I am the Euphrates, and the river is mine. From its upper waters high in the mountains to the marshes where it meets the sea, I am the river. I am every deserted bend and I am the water that flows past the walls of Babylon, crossed with many bridges."

Hadad took a deep breath. "What do you want from me?"

"One night in your arms," she said, "for reasons of my own. If you please me, I will give you a blessing."

Why did Hadad say yes, you may wonder? Perhaps it was that he was all alone on the river in a tiny boat. Perhaps it was that she was beautiful. Perhaps it was fear or desire, but knowing Hadad, it was probably curiosity. He was a very clever young man, you see, and it's not every day that one has the chance to lie with a goddess. It's not the sort of thing you turn down when it comes your way if you've always wondered about everything.

And so he did, and at dawn he rowed home and put his boat away and went into the house and lay down on his bed to sleep. "No catch this morning?" his mother said before he fell into dreams.

"The fish weren't biting," Hadad said.

They were the next day, and the next. His fishing was good. Not ridiculously good, but better than it had been before. He never came home empty-handed, and there was always enough for his mother to sell in the markets of Babylon. Each dawn he would bring home a catch and go to bed while she carried it into the city and sold it, and so they prospered more than they had. If Hadad had hoped for some greater blessing, he was philosophical about it. It had been one night, and if it brought them some good fortune, that was enough. The expression of pinched worry left his mother's face.

One night (and it was a year and a day from the night he met Atargatis, though Hadad had forgotten the exact time) Hadad was fishing in the moonlight when again he heard a *plish*. He turned around quickly in the boat.

She swam toward him holding something above the water. Catching hold of the boat, she handed it to him. Hadad stared at it in shock.

It was a baby girl, not a newborn but about three months old, with soft dark hair and eyes wide open, searching his face thoughtfully. They were the same uncanny gray as her mother's, the color of a sky about to storm.

"Her name is Sammuramat," Atargatis said. "I told you I would give you a blessing. She is not just for you. She is for all of the people of the river."

"It's a baby," Hadad said. It wasn't the brightest thing he ever said, but he was quite surprised.

"She is our daughter," Atargatis said. "And you will raise her and she will fulfill a great purpose. And now, farewell." She bent and kissed her daughter's forehead, and then with a flip of her shining tail, disappeared beneath the water.

"Wait!" Hamad said, but there was no answer. In his arms, Sammuramat regarded him, her forehead wrinkled as if in worry. "Well," Hadad said. He carefully put her between his knees because he would need both hands to get the boat home. "I suppose that's that." He would have some explaining to do to his mother.

His mother took the story quite well, considering. That very morning she went to the markets of Babylon and bought a goat so there would be milk for the baby. "We'll manage," she said. "I've always wanted a granddaughter." And so they did.

As the years passed, Sammuramat grew up along the river, swimming almost before she could walk. She was quick to laugh, clever with her hands braiding nets or baskets, strong and reliable about getting nets in. She grew up long-limbed with dark hair that crackled and snapped when it was brushed out, tanned and bold and unafraid of even the big ships that might overrun an unwary little fishing boat. When she went to the market with her grandmother, it seemed Sammuramat knew everyone and had befriended all, even the jewel merchants who were grumpy and the foreigners who barely spoke a proper word. By the time she was fifteen years old, everyone knew Sammuramat, but she did not let anyone court her. She was slippery as a fish and evaded all advances with a smile.

Now in this time, the king who ruled over Babylon was Sulmanu-asaredu, the Assyrian king who had conquered it when Hadad was a little boy. He was a very rich and great king, with forty-two cities that acknowledged him as ruler and an army of thousands who obeyed his wishes. Talents of gold and silver flowed into his hands as tribute from Damascus to Arabia to Susa and the highlands of the north. He had many children, but his heir was Prince Shamshi, who was nearly eighteen years old.

And so the word went out in the markets of Babylon that King Sulmanu intended to stock the harem for his son when he came of age. There were those who dreaded it and hid their daughters away for fear that they might be chosen, and some girls promptly eloped with boys they loved so they would be disqualified. Others hoped to be picked. After all, would not this give them a life of wealth and ease? When the eunuchs set up great tents in the square before the ancient temple of Ishtar, the daughters of merchants arrived beautifully dressed in litters to present themselves, while the daughters of the poor lined up and watched them.

Sammuramat went with her friends. They pointed to extravagant clothes, girls with gold bracelets around their arms, and the eunuchs who interviewed each one. It was very exciting.

"Wouldn't it be wonderful," one of her friends said, "to never have to work hard again?"

Sammuramat craned her neck to get a better view. "I can't imagine that anyone would work harder than the one chosen by the prince," she said. "Audiences and diplomacy, ambassadors and the treasury. Imagine keeping a house the size of the palace! All the servants who answer to you, and raising your children to be responsible and kind! And not an ordinary husband who worries about catching enough fish, but one who has to worry about whether there will be war and if he makes a bad decision will cities burn and his people die."

At that, a young man who was helping the eunuchs write down the names of likely girls turned his head. He was tall and well-built, though he stooped a little to make himself seem smaller, with the beginnings of a neatly trimmed beard. "You are right," he said. "The prince will make one his wife, the mother of his heir, and no one will have to work harder than she does. But it would also be nice if she could share his burdens and his toil."

"Then he should marry a girl who wants to work," Sammuramat said. "Not a spoiled girl who wants nothing but fancy clothes. And if he cared for her and respected her and treated her well, perhaps she would love him as well as revere him, and his burdens would be lightened."

"You are very wise," he said, and his eyes rested on hers. "Who are you?"

"I am Sammuramat," she said, "daughter of Hadad the fisherman. And I'm not here to get on the list. I don't expect the prince is going to consider the daughter of a fisherman."

"Shamshi might surprise you," he said.

Now you have guessed already, haven't you? The young man was Shamshi himself, pretending to be one of his servants so that he could see the girls without them posturing and showing off the way they would when they met the prince. He was clever too. When he met Sammuramat, he knew that he had found the girl he was looking for. Of course he chose her.

And of course, because this is the kind of story that it is, he came to love her and she came to love him. In a year or two they had a son named Hadad-Nirari, a beautiful little boy who became the heir in turn when Shamshi became king. Sammuramat was his queen and his support in all things, and she in turn was respected and heeded. It might have been that they would have been very happy for a long time and together ruled wisely and well. But of course it was not that simple. When Shamshi had ruled only four years, the Medes invaded. There was a great battle. Hundreds of men died, their bodies left for the kites because they fled the field and could not even bring their dead. One of them was Shamshi, who died bravely with his men in the battle.

Word of the great defeat came to Babylon like a black wind. People ran in the streets from house to house, rending their clothes and putting ashes on their faces. In the halls of the magnificent palace, there was silence. The king was dead and Hadad-Nirari was only five years old—he could not rule a mighty kingdom. He could not lead an army against the Medes. He was just a little boy who was learning his letters and playing with toy animals. "Who will lead us?" people cried. "What will become of us?" They already imagined the great city fallen, people dead in the streets.

Their cries cut through her grief and pain. Sammamurat lifted her head. It was like a wind at her back, the wind that comes before the storm. "I will lead you," she said. She kissed her son and left him in the nursery to play. She put on armor and rode out in a chariot before her men. She lifted a spear to the sky. "I am the

Thunder of Heaven!" she said. "I am the Daughter of the River! Those who try me will fall!"

She knew the numbers of the muster. She knew the generals who led them. She knew the villages that had sent men to the army. She knew the women who waited for them at home. All this she had learned as Shamshi's queen. She had worked for it at his side. Now Sammamurat stood alone.

When the Medes descended on Babylon, they were met with flood and fire. And then, like thunder in the sky, Sammamurat's chariots attacked on their flank. They fled before them in a rout. The Median army was broken. Strategy and courage had won the day.

Sammamurat reigned as her son's regent for thirteen long years. Then she handed the crown to her son and stepped back as his counselor, though Hadad-Nirari listened to her all her life and honored her. He built statues in her honor—his mother, the daughter of Atargatis who had saved her people and reigned over them in peace.

Questions to Consider

Now that you have read a story about Atargatis and her daughter Sammamurat, take out your journaling materials, paper and a writing implement or an electronic means of journaling. It's time to consider your reaction to the story you just read.

- What is your immediate, emotional reaction to the story? How does it make you feel?

- There are many stories of young men who are the sons of a god and who grow up to become heroes who unexpectedly rise to save their people. What did you think of a story of a young woman who is the daughter of a goddess doing the same?

- Why do you think Atargatis decided to have a daughter with Hadad? What was the goddess's purpose? How does this fit with your concept of what a goddess might do?

- What did you think of Atargatis herself? You may be familiar with mermaids, but a river mermaid may be a new idea. What did you think of her as the mermaid goddess of the Euphrates River?

Now that we have read a story in which Atargatis and her daughter figure, let's delve more deeply into Atargatis's worship.

Ancient Worship: Atargatis

In the first chapter of this book, we talked about gods of place. Atargatis is a good example of a god of place who became a universal god.

The Mermaid Goddess

It seems that Atargatis was at first worshiped as the river spirit of the Euphrates River in the likeness of a mermaid. However, around the time of the historical Queen Sammuramat (around 800 BCE), her worship became widespread in the Assyrian Empire.[20] Since statuary and inscriptions date from this period, one can theorize that it reflects the interests of the rulers who favored her worship. However, Atargatis remained an Assyrian fertility goddess, one who perhaps had a complex worship and who was sometimes conflated with Astarte or Ishtar.

---

20. Bilde, "Atargatis," 151–153.

Something changed with the rise of the Seleucid Kingdom right after the death of Alexander the Great, the beginning of the Hellenistic period. Inscriptions and statuary began to spread far from the Assyrian homeland to the Greek island of Delos, to Ptolemais in Egypt, and even to Rome, possibly due to greater mobility. As discussed earlier, when people—especially women—traveled with the armies of the day, they brought their goddesses. However, Atargatis seems to have found fertile ground where her worship was brought, judging from the sheer number of inscriptions discovered. This worship appears to have evolved a mystery tradition with temples that held elaborate rites for initiates.[21]

Was there a deliberate embrace of Atargatis by the Seleucid kings just as the Ptolemies in Egypt embraced Isis? It is possible. Some Seleucid coins produced by the royal mints show Atargatis or Atargatis and Hadad as early as 300 BCE.[22] However, whether that reflected a deliberate desire to spread her worship or was simply a recognition of the place Atargatis already held is unknown. Whatever the reason, her worship did spread. For example, a hundred years later there is a votive inscription from Acre in what is now Israel that reads, "To Hadad and Atargatis, the gods who listen to prayers, Diodotos son of Neoptolemos on behalf of himself and Philista his wife and their children has dedicated this altar in fulfillment of a vow." The inscription is in Greek, as are the names of the dedicators.[23] It is worth pointing out that this does not mean

21. Bilde, "Atargatis," 161–162.

22. Jan Zahle, "Religious Motifs on Seleucid Coins," in *Religion and Religious Practice in the Seleucid Kingdom* (Oxford, UK: Aarhus University Press, 1990), 128.

23. Javier Teixidor, "Interpretations and Misinterpretations of the East in Hellenistic Times" in *Religion and Religious Practice in the Seleucid Kingdom* (Oxford, UK: Aarhus University Press, 1990), 71.

that Diodotos and Philista were Greek in terms of ethnicity. Just as in the modern-day United States where many people have English names but are not of English heritage, the same was true in the Hellenistic world of Greek names. If someone's name is John, it doesn't mean they're of English ancestry or European descent. Diodotos and Philista might have been Greek or they simply had Greek names because that was the dominant culture.

It's possible to read the inscription as evidence that Atargatis's worship spread beyond her original boundaries, or that people who had Hellenized names continued to worship as their ancestors had. We cannot know which is true. It is likely, however, that both scenarios were true of some people in this period when peoples and gods mingled so freely.

It is certainly true that like the Ptolemies in Egypt, the Seleucid kings attempted to adapt to the peoples they ruled rather than the other way around. For example, the same priestly families continued to hold office in Babylon and other cities throughout the entire period with no disruption. One scholar says that they made "their rule as Babylonian as possible and therefore as easy as possible for Babylonians to experience."[24] In other words, it was different from nineteenth-century colonialism, where the temporal rulers attempted to enforce cultural and religious change on a population. It was an entirely different model where the rulers deliberately adopted religious and cultural features of the ruled. The result was a rich and syncretic culture where people could "sample" both traditions freely.

Atargatis is part of this picture. Her worship was accepted and embraced by the Seleucids, which gave it an opportunity to reach

---

24. Texidor, "Interpretations," 73.

far beyond the area where she originated. By the Roman period, worship of Atargatis as Dea Sura had spread as far as France. Perhaps we should see her, half woman and half fish, as a symbol of syncretism itself. Sammamurat, the daughter of a goddess and a mortal man, is not neither but both, just as her mother is both of the sea and of the land. Through Sammamurat, Atargatis protects her people. But who are her people? They are not people of a particular blood or even of a particular place. Her people are her worshipers. That's it and that's all. To belong to her, what you have to do is join.

Like the other new syncretic religions of the Hellenistic world, people were not judged based on their social status, the color of their skin, or who their grandparents are. We don't know these facts about Diodotos and Philista because it didn't matter; it wasn't relevant. What mattered was that they worshiped Atargatis.

Thunder of Heaven

There are many stories of a young man who discovers that he is secretly the son of a god and therefore destined for heroism. With Sammuramat and Atargatis, we have a young woman who is the daughter of a goddess and therefore has a destiny as the wise ruler and leader of her people.

Let's talk about Sammuramat as a ruling queen. Her story parallels the story of heroes who become kings—she is conceived by a god and an ordinary person, raised in obscurity with little indication of her divine ancestry, and then recognized and raised to power based on her personal attributes. In Sammuramat's case, those attributes are her intellect, her work ethic, and her willingness and skill to take on the complex job of ruling. She is not born a princess—she earns her royal status as a result of her desire to do the job rather than simply enjoy the rewards. Then, as now, ruling is hard work.

Once she has a position of responsibility, Sammuramat delivers. She is a hardworking and conscientious queen, a partner to her husband who rules alone when he is tragically killed. As queen, she rallies the Assyrian troops and saves Babylon from being looted and burned, and then proceeds to rule as a model of wisdom and restraint for thirteen years. And then, rather than engaging in court intrigue or attempting to extend her regency, she turns the rule over to her son when he comes of age. She remains at his side to counsel him for the rest of her life. Her story is blissfully free of scandals, murders, and betrayals. She is not the wicked queen but the wise one.

What can we learn from her story? We are often uncomfortable with women in positions of authority who simply rule well. We are more comfortable with moral authority, when women claim the right to speak based on being better or more moral than those with power. But what about when women have power? How do you wield power if you, yourself, are a woman? Sammuramat's story gives us hints.

Sammuramat does not disguise her femininity. She is a wife, a mother, *and* a queen. Power does not come with masculine identity— she can wield power without being king. Too often, today women are told not to have pictures of their families on their desks. I have been told to cut my long hair and not wear nail polish because appearing too feminine in the workplace "made people think I wasn't very smart." Sammuramat's story reminds us that it is possible to be both feminine *and* powerful.

Second, Sammuramat has worked hard and that work pays off. She knows the people who will be instrumental in securing victory and the peace that follows. She does not rely on blood or beauty to succeed. Like many women in high places today, she has learned the ropes until she mastered them. We are more used to stories of princesses who achieve power at a very young age because of who their fathers are and treat it as a great good that they are naïve and, outside of the mechanisms of power, know very little. And yet we don't treat it as a great good if a young man is ignorant or unqualified. It's not proof of his moral purity that he's in a position he's not qualified for. Sammuramat works hard to qualify for her position, and when the power is hers, she uses it wisely. She is not a pure child. She is a grown woman, a widow, and a mother who has learned about the kingdom she rules. Perhaps it's time to celebrate the achievements of women who have earned their place rather than virtuous virgins who are exalted based on their innocence instead of their experience.

Meeting Atargatis: A Meditation

This meditation may be done in two different ways: Find a partner to read it to you and take turns doing the meditation, or simply read it in a quiet place or even record it and play it to yourself.

You will need a quiet place where you won't be disturbed for twenty minutes or so. You may play soft music if you like. If you have music you normally use while meditating, you may certainly use it. If you would like to use incense, consider one of the recommendations in the correspondences section at the end of this chapter.

This may be an intense experience. Read through the meditation before you begin and decide if it is something you want to do.

Take a deep breath to help you relax. Then take another. Now begin either reading to yourself or listening as the meditation is read to you. If you are having it read to you, close your eyes. Otherwise, read aloud slowly so that you have time to absorb the words.

It's evening and you are walking through a beautiful garden. There are banks of flowering plants, a pleasant breeze blowing, and the scent of the flowers wafts over you. A trellis makes a gate into another part of the garden, jasmine climbing both sides and wreathing over it, white flowers fragrant in the night. You walk through. You hear the sound of running water as the path through the garden leads among islands of greenery.

It's not a fountain or a pool. The garden leads down to the bank of a little river. There are benches and comfortable places to stop, places where you can look out over the water. The sky is bright with stars. It's a lovely place. You pause, enjoying the peaceful view.

You hear a sound: plish! *You look around.*

She has surfaced not far from the bank, Atargatis, the Mermaid Queen. Her long hair is silver, and when she swims one green fluke of her tail surfaces for a moment above the water. She's beautiful. You've never seen anyone so breathtakingly sublime. When she raises herself up on the bank and smiles at you, you are overwhelmed.

"So quiet?" Atargatis asks. "When you have come to see me and I have come to see you?"

You reply, telling her that you are glad to meet her.

"And I am glad to meet you," she says. "At last." She holds out a crown. It's a gold circlet meant to fit on your brow. "This is for you."

A crown? For you? "I think you must be mistaken," you say.

She shakes her head. "A crown is a symbol of power. Tell me about the power your wield, or may wield."

Perhaps that's easy. You hold a position of responsibility in society. You have employees who answer to you, students, subordinates, people who you may reward or punish. Maybe it's promoting or firing. Maybe it's giving them grades. Maybe lives are literally in your hands as a medical professional or first responder. You have the power to change the course of someone's life each day.

Or maybe you don't think about your power because society doesn't value it so much—you teach young children and change the course of their lives or care for children or others in need as a caregiver. Maybe you build things that people use, make clothing, or landscape property, build sidewalks, or install appliances, and you don't see those things as having power—unless people don't have them. Then, they feel your power clearly.

Or perhaps your power is intangible. You draw or write, you draw up wills and documents, or work in the studio of a TV station. You influence, and influencing is power. You create or present things that change lives.

Unless you are too young, you wield power to a greater or lesser extent. It's part of being an adult with adult responsibilities. If you are too young, you will wield this power in a few years. What will you do with it?

Atargatis smiles. She understands what you have been thinking. "What kind of ruler are you?" she asks.

Tell her. Tell her what values inspire your work. Tell her what you are working for. This may be easy or it may be difficult if you have not thought about this before. Try to be honest with the goddess. What are your strengths? Are you hardworking? Inspirational? Quick-witted? Competent? Creative? Highly skilled? Tell her *how you rule others. Are you fair? Open-minded? Firm with people who need guidance? Patient? Stern? Different work requires different kinds of ruling, just as it requires different physical skills. Atargatis understands all of this.*

When you have finished, she regards you. The water circulates around her, making a soothing sound. "What do you need to be a better ruler?" she asks. "Tell me, and I will help you."

You think about it and then tell her what you need. Maybe it's a skill. Maybe it's a quality, such as more patience. It is something that you honestly hope to cultivate in yourself that will make you better at wielding the power you have.

"Take the crown," she says, "and wear it as a symbol of the rule you have, and of the ruler you hope to be. The world is made by humans, by people like you. You matter. Your choices matter, and your power is real."

You bend and let her put it on your brow. Maybe it feels strange there. Maybe it feels good. "Thank you," you say.

Atargatis smiles again. "Go," she says, "but know that you can always find me here if you wish to talk. I am happy to offer you counsel."

Wearing the circlet, you begin to make your way back through the garden, away from the riverbank. When you look back, all you see is the broad expanse of flowing water. The goddess has departed.

You walk between the banks of flowers until you reach the jasmine-studded arch. You walk through. From there it's just a short walk home as the garden fades around you and you return to normal consciousness.

When you are fully back, turn off any music and put out any incense. Think for a moment about your experience. How do you feel? This may have been a very intense meditation. You may wish to ground by eating or drinking. You may want to take a shower to help return to the physical present.

What did it feel like to be asked about power? Are you comfortable thinking of yourself as powerful? How do you feel about seeing yourself as a ruler? If you are journaling, you may wish to write about this experience. Take the time you need to process it.

Lessons from Atargatis: The Mermaid Queen

Now that we have done a meditation to meet Atargatis, let's talk a little bit more about her gifts and how we can incorporate them into our lives. Her gifts are courage, curiosity, and hard work.

Courage

Often when we think of courage we think of physical bravery, like Sammuramat showed when she led her army to victory. That is one kind of courage. However, that wasn't the first time or the first way in which she showed bravery. It required as much or more courage to change her life entirely by marrying Shamshi and taking on enormous responsibility. The audacity to go somewhere new, to take a job outside your comfort zone, to talk to someone new, to challenge yourself to take on responsibilities that seem awesome—these are all kinds of courage. It's a kind that is often unrecognized, but one that surely changes our lives.

In my own life, one of the scariest things I've ever done was walk up to the director of a national organization, a woman I'd met once before, and ask her to hire me for an important job, a lobbying job that would require relocating to DC and playing on a national political field. Know what? She hired me. Part of the reason was that I dared ask. If I wouldn't dare ask her, how would I dare ask members of Congress to vote for bills? Lots of people want to change their lives, but having the courage to actually take the step is hard. It deserves to be appreciated. Courage doesn't have to involve running into burning buildings; it can be about choosing to do things that are intimidating.

When you step outside your comfort zone and take a chance, you are displaying courage, whether it's related to a job, school, or personal relationships. For example, it's hard to make new friends. People can be mean; they can reject you. Making friendly overtures to people can be misinterpreted. And yet if we all simply sat in our houses alone, the world would be a poorer place for us all. Reaching out to others requires courage, especially if you've been hurt. However, as with many things, the potential rewards are so great that the chance is worth it. I had a friend years ago who had been through a painful breakup. He wouldn't take a chance on meeting anyone he might be interested in because he feared it would be the same old story. And yet if he didn't, he would never have an opportunity to have a better relationship. The woman of his dreams wasn't already in his house—he had to make some effort to meet her.

Atargatis recognizes audacity. She likes people like Hadad, who see something new and unfamiliar and scary and who leap at the chance.

Curiosity

The other thing that Hadad had that endeared him to Atargatis was curiosity. He could have turned down her proposal. He could have said "no thanks" and gone on having an ordinary life. Instead, he chose to be a goddess's lover with all the transformation that included. He wondered what would happen, He wanted to know what it would be like.

Today, we have so many voices urging us to caution in every part of our lives. That's understandable. When the world is a scary place, it's easy for everything to seem too perilous to dare. The voice that speaks against caution is often curiosity; What would happen if I did...? What would it be like to live in a different country? What would it be like to date someone completely different from anyone I've known? What would it be like to take a foster child into my home? To travel somewhere off the beaten track? To spend time with people in my community who are different from me?

We are in a part of a cultural cycle that encourages us to gather in, stay close to home, and take few personal chances. We're even actively told that curiosity is bad—we should instead "stay in our lane." And yet, it's hard to grow within carefully circumscribed boundaries. Curiosity leads us to wonder what's over the fence. Maybe it's bad, but maybe it's good. Maybe it's both. In any event, going over the fence is often necessary for further growth. If we give ourselves permission to explore, we are giving ourselves permission to find new interests, new people, and transform ourselves and the world around us.

Hard Work

The other thing that was key to Sammamurat's success was her hard work. Curiosity led her to watch the selection of brides for Prince Shamshi even though she had no intention of competing. Courage led her to take a chance on him, marry him and change her life. But the unglamourous part of the story is the years she spent working hard and learning how to be queen. Ruling queens aren't born; they're made. Ruling is a craft like any other. That's why the old term is "statecraft." It's not about talent or inherent goodness or anything else except learning how the sausage is made and how to make it.

This is true of many fields of endeavor. Talent and courage can get a foot in the door, but solid work has to back it up. It's great to register for classes at a university, but then you have to go to class and do the work. It's one thing to get a job and another to excel at it for years. Lots of people struggle with this; they start strong but then fade at the test. Can you really keep doing it well when the first rush of curiosity is over?

Atargatis is the patron of ruling queens because she understands and appreciates the hard work of statecraft. Sammamurat is the model of the ruling queen: just, brave, and above all, hardworking. Courage saves the kingdom. Hard work runs it. As you think about the next rite, consider what you might want Atargatis's help with in your life. What do you need to work hard on to stick the landing?

Ruling Queens

Let's stop for a moment and think about what we mean by ruling queens. Lots of times what we imagine is a beautiful woman whose only job is to be attractive and have babies while her husband does all the realm's work. While that was occasionally true in history, most of the time it wasn't. Most queens, like Sammamurat, had a lot of work to do; at the very least, they managed the palace.

Think about the job of White House Chief of Staff. It's one of the most important jobs in Washington. Running the White

House, managing the President's schedule, appearances, media coverage, and the day-to-day operations of the hundreds of people who work in the White House is an enormous job. That's the queen's job, what the queen has done in many states for thousands of years. Even if she theoretically had no policy responsibility and didn't lead armies, she was the Chief of Staff. Only very rarely has the role of queen meant sitting around in pretty clothes. Most queens had responsibilities to fulfill, and their failure to fulfill them was a catastrophe. Taking on the energy of a ruling queen does not mean being passive or selfish, it means being the Chief of Staff: competent, hardworking, knowledgeable, and a superlative manager.

A Rite to Honor Atargatis

This rite to honor Atargatis involves asking her to help you with something you are working on and helping you embody the power of the ruling queen. Like Sammamurat, you can accept power and wield it wisely, a difficult concept for some people. Atargatis can help you claim your power.

This rite is designed for one person but can be adapted if you wish to do it with others. If you are doing this with multiple people, each one will need a symbol of their work: it could be a charm or statuette or something taken with you to your workplace: a patch, a badge, or something that belongs on a desk—whatever symbolizes your work to you. For example, if you are a nurse, you might use a pin that symbolizes your profession, or something such as your work ID on a lanyard. It may be something you treasure, like your diploma, or it may be something as simple as a mug that reads "World's Greatest Nurse." It should be something that you can take with you to the place where you work.

You Will Need

- An image of Atargatis or a mermaid of any kind
- The charm or other object you intend to use (if you have more than one person, you will need one each)
- A blue, aqua, or turquoise candle of any size or shape
- Incense and a burner (preferably rose, jasmine, lotus, or sandalwood)
- A small pitcher of wine or fruit juice
- A goblet or cup
- A libation bowl

Optional Extras

- A plate of cucumbers or melons cut into bite-sized pieces
- A plate for food offerings if you are using them
- Paper and a writing implement
- A blue or green altar cloth

First, arrange your altar to Atargatis. Place the image in the center back, and then group the other items pleasingly around it. You may add other embellishments if you wish—more candles, more images, elaborate and fancy dishes to hold the food and drink. It is appropriate to use your best. It is also appropriate to dress in Atargatis's colors for this rite: aqua, blue, turquoise, green, and/or white. It is also appropriate to wear clothes that represent the work you do, if you have specific clothes that you wear.

Since you are directly petitioning a goddess rather than working a spell or performing a large ritual, you will not need to perform a quarter calling. It is not necessary to call upon deities other than the one you are petitioning.

Prepare by turning off electronic devices or electric lights and putting yourself in a reflective frame of mind. If you are playing music, start it now.

Light the candle and then the incense if you are using it. Say, "Atargatis, Mermaid Queen of the Great River, I call to you to honor you. I call to you to know you. I call to you to ask for your blessing."

Pour wine into the cup. Then pour a libation into the bowl for the goddess and take a sip from the cup yourself. Say, "As you were honored long ago, so I (we) honor you today. I (we) sing your praises. I (we) tell your story. I (we) do not forget you, doubled Lady, goddess in both air and water."

If you are using a food offering of cucumbers or melons, present the plate and put a few pieces in the offering dish. Say, "Please accept these gifts of earth and water. I (we) present them to you so that we may share in the bounty of the world." Eat a small piece of the melon or cucumber yourself.

Say, "Please hear the story of my striving." Then tell Atargatis about the work you do in your life where you wield power or hope to wield power in the future: It could be a job, an artistic endeavor, or caregiving. Think carefully about the responsibilities you have and about the effect you have on others. For example, if you are a gatekeeper who vets others' work or who hires or evaluates interns, you have direct responsibility for who has opportunities in their career. That is a very great power. Take some time to tell Atargatis about the seriousness of this power and your concerns about using it wisely.

If you are very young and do not have any responsibilities that affect others, think about a time in the future when you will. If you are an intern yourself, one day you will be the boss. If you are a student training for a profession, one day you will be working in that profession with the responsibilities it entails. At some point in your life, you will also likely have responsibility for someone else, whether a child, an aging parent, a partner who is ill, or friends who depend on you. How will you handle the responsibility of caregiving? What kind of ruler do you want to be?

Bear in mind that Atargatis wants you to use your power wisely. She will not be impressed by the desire to use power for self-aggrandizement or hurting others. She is the patron of the ruling queen and conscientious ruler, not the tyrant. She will not appreciate the expression of power for revenge, even if couched in the appropriated language of justice, e.g., "they deserve to hurt because they're bad."

The other thing to consider in your petition to Atargatis is the size of your request. "I want to bring about world peace and end all forms of injustice anywhere" is a laudable goal, but it is also impossible. Focus your efforts on goals that are within the scope of your work. "I would like to get the Missouri legislature to prohibit employment discrimination on the basis of gender identity." "I would like to make sure that every foster child in my county has a placement that respects their right to practice their own religion." "I would like to relieve people's pain and improve their health through my work as a dental hygienist." One of the easiest ways to sabotage success is to make the goal unattainable. Ask for Atargatis's help with a goal that is something you can meaningfully affect.

Think about how you might achieve your goal. Take time and let inspiration touch you as you wait in sacred space. Sometimes thinking about things differently and with focus will help you. Sometimes Atargatis will touch you with inspiration and you will find yourself thinking about your goal differently than you originally did, or a path may become clear to you. If it does not, keep your eyes and mind open in the next days. Sometimes it takes time for you to see paths that are open. Or perhaps you are already on the path! If, for example, you are currently working as a teacher and your hope is to be a truly inspirational teacher who changes lives, you may already be doing what you need to do. What you need is encouragement to keep going, not a change of trajectory. Keep in mind that if you do not see a shift ahead of you, it may simply not be necessary. You may already be doing the work of a good ruler.

If you are doing this ritual with more than one person, make sure each person gets a chance to speak about their goal and then let everyone think about it at the same time. If people do not feel comfortable speaking their goals aloud, they may write them on paper and lay the paper on the altar.

When you have finished thinking about how you will be a wise ruler and have given Atargatis time to speak, thank her:

"Atargatis, Mermaid Queen, thank you for your time and your counsel. You are the mother of heroes, the mother of queens, patron of wise rulers. Dea Sura, Lady of the River, I appreciate your care. Please be with me as I carry out my responsibilities to the best of my ability. Please let this item be a focus for your power and for mine."

Place your fingertips on the item you selected to put on the altar, whatever it may be. Feel Atargatis's favor passing through you and into the item, charging it with her energy. This may take a few moments or a few minutes. Allow it to take as long as it needs, maintaining your focus on the work you wish to do. When you feel that you are finished, say, "Thank you, Gracious Lady, for your time and your favor."

Blow out the candles and the incense if you are using it. Take the symbol of your work, which you have charged, and keep it with you. You may wear it, carry it in a pocket, or put it on an altar or in a place where you will see or use it at work.

Take the libation bowl outside and pour it out on the ground. If you have a food offering of cucumber or melon, leave it outside.

As you take down the altar, thank Atargatis again for her care. Watch for her hand in the days to come.

Atargatis' Correspondences

Here are some correspondences to help you honor Atargatis, whether it's setting up an altar to her, planning a ritual that invokes her, or simply bringing some of her energy into your daily life.

Colors: Blue, green, aqua, turquoise, and gray (water and sky is the theme)

Incense: Jasmine, rose, sandalwood

Symbols: The trident

Festival Day: When the sun enters Pisces, about February 18, or alternately the full moon of February

Food: cucumber, melons

Chapter Six

Epona, Lady of Horses

Today, Epona is thought of as a goddess native to the British Isles or sometimes northern France as well. However, the Celtic tribes of the Hellenistic period were spread across Europe, as far east as the Black Sea and what is now Romania. They fought wars into Greece in 281–279 BCE and migrated into northern Turkey in 278, where they established the Kingdom of Galatia.[25] Celts also lived in the Hellenistic kingdoms of Pontus and Pergamon, and smaller groups of soldiers took service with many of the successor states, thus mingling with far-flung peoples. Apuleius tells us that there was a shrine to Epona in Alexandria.

This is a story that might have been told about how those migrations came to pass.

25. Ian Barnes, *The Historical Atlas of the Celtic World* (New York: Chartwell, 2009), 40–43.

Story: Beli and the Wicked Prince

Once, long ago but not so long as all that, in the time of our great-grandmothers, there was a very wicked prince. He was the heir of a kingdom far away, and he was so wicked that when he was but fourteen years old he beat his horse blind because it had not carried him to victory in a race with other boys. You gasp because this is very wicked indeed. It was, and even in that country, among people who understand little of honor as we know it, this was a shocking crime. It was so shocking that his father, who was a wise and just king, said that he would have no horse since he mistreated his, and he would go on foot like a slave rather than a prince.

Yes, that was well done, and if he had learned from it, it would have been well. But this prince was called Thunderbolt, because from his earliest days he had been given to rages and sudden storms, his tantrums falling like spears of lightning upon the household. They did not live as we do, men and women together, and women lived apart in their own rooms of the great house. Thunderbolt was the king's eldest son, and his mother was young and fair and well-born, but she was not a forceful person and had not disciplined him in childhood, so now he was a youth accustomed to having his own way, which his father would have none of. Therefore his father resolved that Thunderbolt would not be king after him, for if he could not govern himself he would not govern their people well.

Now Thunderbolt had a younger half-brother, fully eight years his junior, and he was a scholar instead of a warrior. Thunderbolt scoffed at him, for as he grew his body was keen and his temper well suited to arms, and he became a warrior of some note. He called his brother soft and useless, for he preferred books to spears. He was quite sure he was his father's heir, you see. And yet the more his temper and his pride grew, the more determined his father was that he should never be king.

What has this to do with us? I will come to that in a moment. But you should know by now how he had offended her, the Lady of Horses, Epona who guards our herds and our homes. He had blinded a horse for no reason, and he had beaten and mistreated them in his rages. He had offended her, and her eye was already upon him, for like the lead mare when she sees a lion in the mountains, she is implacable in defending what is hers.

As soon as his brother was old enough, the king made Thunderbolt's brother his heir instead of Thunderbolt, and Thunderbolt left the kingdom, determined to win a greater one elsewhere. First he went to the Kingdom of Macedon where his half-sister, Arsinoë, ruled as queen, wed to an old man who was their father's friend, but he found a chilly welcome there.

Next he went to the land of the Seleucids, where Seleucus the First still ruled over his people. "There is an easy war to win," he said, "against my sister and her husband. Her husband is an old man and their sons are children. We can take the kingdom easily." And so Seleucus made war, and Thunderbolt stood at his side, and his sister's husband was slain in battle.

"We have triumphed," Seleucus said. "When we have taken the kingdom from your sister, it will be yours."

Very wicked indeed, yes. But Thunderbolt was wickeder still. The thought came to him: why should he have one kingdom when he might have two? When he sat with Seleucus in his tent, near as a son, he stabbed the old general and killed him, bound as he was by guest-friendship. Then he proclaimed himself king of all Seleucus' realm.

You are right, he did not get away with it! Seleucus' men would have none of it, and Seleucus had a son, Antiochus, who was a strong man in middle age, and they turned on Thunderbolt with swift revenge. Thunderbolt fled. He went to his sister's kingdom, the widowed Arsinoë whose husband he had slain in battle, and he went to her with honeyed words. "It was all Seleucus's doing," he said. "It was not my desire to leave your three little boys orphans. Since I have been the inadvertent reason why they have no father, let me be a father to them. I will hold the kingdom for them until they are grown and I will call them my sons. I will marry you and be your strong right hand."

His sister! Yes, his own half-sister. Now they did such things in some foreign places, but this shocked her nearly as much as it shocks you. She was still young and quite beautiful, you see. But there was Thunderbolt's army, oath-bound to him, and there stood the Seleucids who made war, and she had been away from her brother a long time and did not know him as well as she might. And so she agreed. Perhaps she was afraid. Perhaps she trusted him. But Arsinoë agreed. Her oldest son was fostered away, but she went to Cassandreia with the younger two, garlanded for a wedding. They were wed, and on the third day after he took his half-sister to the marriage bed, he killed her two little boys and left their bodies unburied for the kites, and would not even let their mother touch them or wash them.

Her screams went up to the heavens. "Hear me, any goddess who will! See what has been done! Avenge me! Avenge my babies. My babies...."

Epona heard her. When Arsinoë screamed in Cassandreia, our Lady of Horses heard her. She loves children, you know, as she loves foals, and she is no gentle goddess but lady of the wild places, of the far pastures and endless plains where storms come like towers of cloud over ripening grass. Epona knew that now Thunderbolt controlled this kingdom, Macedon, which lay on the edge of our lands. The tribes had come over the Danu three generations earlier, and while they paid tribute to Philip when he ruled there and his bright son as well, they had sacked Seuthopolis not long since, and they had won the seashore and the harbors for bright trade ships. Epona did not want cruel Thunderbolt for our neighbor.

Now there was a warrior of our people, Beli, who was as temperate as Thunderbolt was angry. When he was just a child he had been given his name, "Little Bel," because he was a shining, sunny child who cared for the responsibilities he was given. When he was ten, he had a horse of his own because his father was of high blood, and he rode it well. Yet once when his father went out to see what he was doing in some boys' game, he found that Beli and his two friends were taking turns riding the horse. "Why do you let them ride your horse?" he asked.

Beli answered, "We're practicing for the trimarkisia, which always takes three friends." Now that is a tactic our men take in battle where three riders share—one fights on horseback, one prepares a horse for battle, and one prepares for battle himself. Therefore, if the fighter or his horse is wounded, a fresh horse or a fresh rider steps up and enters the fray. Thus our charges never falter. Beli showed then that he understood that we are only as strong as we are when we stand together, and that mean spirits result in losses. Understand this—a king is only as great as his honor. Beli understood this, though he was no king. We did not have them in those days, only leaders who deserved their place and who won it through prowess or wisdom.

Now Beli was of an age with Thunderbolt, and by the time that wicked prince had made himself king of Macedon Beli was a war-leader of our people, one of three with Brennus and Acichorius, and the Macedonians called him Belgios. These three war-leaders came together and they considered the problem.

"Macedon has long been a great kingdom," Brennus said, "but now it is weak."

Acichorius said, "There will never be a better time to press southward. We must consolidate what we have won or they will retake the coastal cities and we will be cut off again from the trade with the Inner Sea."

Beli said, "And we have Thunderbolt on our southern border, and he will attack us as soon as he is able. He will not stick to the borders as Lysimachus did before him, or Cassandros before that, or Alexander before him, who kept faith with us when we abjured the Great King of Persia. We cannot let such a man be king, or we will be forever waiting for lightning to strike."

So it was decided and so it was that we swept southward into Macedon with sword and flame, and Epona's hooves were heard in that land which had for so long claimed dominion over others. Beli met Thunderbolt in battle. Thunderbolt rode upon a great beast, an elephant from a far kingdom, because no horse would bear him. His men had shining spears and their phalanx was great, but we buzzed about them like flies, our horsemen advancing and retreating, until they were tired with marching and counter-marching in the sun. Then Beli fell upon them in truth, and Thunderbolt fell from his great beast and his men routed.

As the sun set, Thunderbolt was brought before Beli, and still he was arrogant. "I will not bend," he said, "to a barbarian such as you. I am the king and the son of a king."

"You rule a kingdom you usurped through the murder of children," Beli said sternly. "Your own father would not have you, and your brother rules his kingdom instead. You have angered the gods in every way and you have forfeited all honor that you might claim through your misdeeds. The blood of innocents calls out to Epona for vengeance, and she shall have it!"

He ordered Thunderbolt's head struck off and it was mounted on a spear so that all might see what had transpired. That was the end of the wicked prince.

And Epona whispered to Beli, "Your work is done. Go home to your fields and your family, for if you continue on you will do more than justice requires."

Beli heeded the goddess, and he and his men returned home. However, Brennus and Acichorius did not, and they sacked Delphi and stole talents of gold and silver from the god who dwelled there, bringing down a mighty curse upon themselves, but Beli was not there. The curse, and all that came from it is another story, but Beli's story ends well. He ruled long in Histria opening trade all over the Inner Sea and treating with many kinds of men. It was in his day that some even went to Egypt with their horses to serve Pharaoh, who was by then the nephew of Thunderbolt, and they took Epona with them. That is why she has a shrine in white Alexandria by the sea.

We call him Beli Mawr, Beli the Great, and his tribe has taken his name and call themselves the Belgae, the children of Beli. He served Epona all his life. He knew her, you see, and he knew that what she calls us to is stewardship, to tend our herds wisely and well, to fight fiercely at need, and to live with honor. May we also know her blessings.

Questions to Consider

Now that you have read a story about Epona, take out your journaling materials, either paper and a writing implement, or an electronic means of journaling. It's time to consider your reaction to the story you just read.

- What is your immediate, emotional reaction to Epona's story?

- What do you think of Beli and why he won the goddess's favor? What kind of hero is he to his people? What do you think of Arsinoë? Why do you think Epona listened to her prayer for justice?

- Why would Epona appeal to people outside of her original Celtic tribes? Why do you think her worship spread? Is she a goddess you would be comfortable invoking? Why or why not?

- Were you familiar with Epona before? How does her portrayal in this story match what you already thought? How is it different?

Ancient Worship: Epona

We do not entirely know how Epona was worshiped in ancient times. The Celts she originates with left no written records in this period, so what we do know was written by people who came into contact with them. From Apuleius and others we know that her worship was carried around the Mediterranean and that there was a shrine to her in Alexandria. There was even a little shrine to her in the royal stables of the palace there. Perhaps it was set up by men who had come as soldiers in the service of Pharaoh. As discussed earlier, the Ptolemies allowed all worship in Alexandria, so a shrine to Epona would not have been out of place.

Lady of Horses

Images have been found all over the Hellenistic world. She is usually portrayed as either mounted on a mare or accompanied by a mare or mare and foal. Interestingly, she is rarely shown with any kind of armor or weapon—Epona is not a warrior goddess. She is a protector and guardian of horses, herds, and the people who depend on them, not a goddess of battle or patron of soldiers. It is theorized that she is an aspect of an originally Indo-European horse goddess, since her name means "Divine Horse."[26] It is possible that the chalk hill-figure of a horse carved into the turf at Uffington in England was in honor of Epona. Sometimes she was also shown with a dog (usually a herding type), a natural part of her role as protector of herds. She is also shown feeding or tending to horses or dogs.

In short, Epona is a goddess of community and work. She is social, like the herds she guards. She is a guardian of relations with others, and especially of the protective functions that allow society to be safe and happy.

Epona gets her hands dirty. She does the hard and thankless work of mucking out stables so that her horses have a clean and healthy place to live. She pitches hay and delivers foals. She cleans up manure and carries big bags of feed. She cleans tack and trims

---

26. Prudence Jones and Nigel Pennick, *A History of Pagan Europe* (New York: Barnes and Noble Books, 1995), 86–87.

hooves. And she rides, companion to the horses she loves, her dog loping along beside.

Meeting Epona: A Meditation

This meditation may be done in two different ways: Find a partner to read it to you and take turns doing the meditation, or simply read it in a quiet place or even record it and play it to yourself.

You will need a quiet place where you won't be disturbed for twenty minutes or so. You may play soft music if you like. If you have music you normally use while meditating, you may certainly use it. If you would like to use incense, consider one of the recommendations in the correspondences section at the end of this chapter.

This may be an intense experience. Read through the meditation before you begin and decide if it is something you want to do.

Take a deep breath to help you relax. Then take another. Now begin either reading to yourself or listening as the meditation is read to you. If you are having it read to you, close your eyes. Otherwise, read aloud slowly so that you have time to absorb the words.

You are walking across green, rolling hills. It's springtime and everything is beautiful. You can feel the warm sun on your skin, though the breeze is cool and comfortable. Wildflowers dot the grass which rises nearly to your knees. This is no golf course or mowed lawn. This is a wild prairie. Bees buzz from flower to flower. High in the air above you a hawk turns on the wind, watching for little animals in the long grass.

You reach the top of the hill and look down. In the little valley between hills and on the opposite slope, a herd of horses is graz-

ing. There are fifteen or so, sleek with new spring coats. Three foals gambol beside their mothers. A yearling is running for the joy of it, racing across the new grass as though the wind was her stablemate. A heavily pregnant mare munches head down in the middle of the herd. On the other hillside, a beautiful bay stallion keeps watch, his head silhouetted against the sky.

You stop, not wanting to frighten them. You stand still and watch, so beautiful, so graceful in their freedom.

"Amazing, aren't they?" You turn. There's a woman standing behind you. She's wearing jeans and a t-shirt and good solid dirty boots, her hair in braids. She smiles and you know her. This is Epona, the Lady of Horses. She looks like she's come from mucking out, none too clean and plenty horsey, her hands dirty with the work of caring for her charges.

"They are beautiful," you say.

"They're a lot of work," she says. "Anything worth doing is." Epona looks at you keenly. "Tell me about your work. What do you do that you're proud of?"

You may have to think before you answer, or you may answer right away. Standing on the hillside in the sunshine, watching the horses grazing, it's easier to think about your work than you expected. Maybe it's your job or maybe it isn't, but it's work you're proud of: the things you do with your hands that make something beautiful or make the world a better place or that take care of some person or creature that needs you. The work you do to soothe, protect, improve, or delight—you tell Epona all about it. You don't have to be shy. You don't have to worry if you're boring her. You can tell her all about the thing you're passionate about at length. She wants to hear.

Or maybe you find yourself telling her about something you want to do. Maybe there's a project or an endeavor you wish you could do or that you miss doing. Maybe it's something that you've heard about and are thinking about doing, or an idea that occurred to you that hasn't come to fruition yet. You tell her about it.

Epona nods. She listens. She asks you questions about what you're excited about. She asks you, "Why do you do this?"

That's a more complicated question and you think about it before you answer. Why do you do it? Love? Hope? Curiosity? To see if it can be done? Compassion? There are as many reasons as people and all of them are right.

Maybe you find yourself telling her about the barriers. You'd do something, only there are reasons you aren't. You don't have the right qualifications. You don't have the right people in your life. You're not able to because of where you live or your age or your health. Epona listens. She doesn't judge. She just listens. You know she's thinking of ways to break down the barriers, but she won't push you. She'll help you if you ask, but she won't make you feel guilty because you haven't done something yet. She's a patient trainer. She understands that you don't take a young horse out and clear a five-foot jump on the first day. You work up to it. First you defeat the fear. You take it one step at a time.

When you are done telling her, she nods. "Well," she says, "it looks like you've got your work cut out for you."

That's comforting. She doesn't tell you that you shouldn't love what you love or want what you want. She doesn't tell you that you should already have succeeded magnificently. She praises the work. She respects what you're doing. Standing here beside her in the sun, watching her horses graze, you feel peace. You can absorb some of her quiet confidence.

"You'll be okay," she says. She smiles. "If you want to talk to me again, you can always come back."

"Thank you," you say. You take a last look at the herd, then turn and start down the hill you climbed up.

When you get to the bottom, you are back in your own place and time. You open your eyes. When you are fully back, turn off any music and put out any incense. Think for a moment about your experience. What did it feel like? How do you feel now?

Lessons from Epona: Lady of Horses

Now that you've read a story about Epona and done a meditation to meet her, let's talk a little bit about her gifts.

Teamwork

As we saw in the story of Beli, one of Epona's great gifts is teamwork. She is not a goddess of solitary heroics, but of working together. Beli wins her approval as well as his father's when he shares his horse with his friends, learning to work together to overcome the enemy. Thunderbolt abused a horse because he didn't beat his friends in a race. Beli shared his horse so that everyone got a turn and succeeded together.

Our society emphasizes competition: "The Best Book of the Year!" "The Best Chicken Recipe!" "The Greatest Song!"—all of these things are false. The best book, recipe, or song are all matters of taste. Maybe you like chicken one way and somebody else likes it another way. That's the way it's supposed to be, but our society sets up intense and false competitions by giving prizes and accolades for "the best" when often times there is no best. There's only what you prefer.

Forced competition has terrible consequences. For example, when I was starting writing I had a somewhat more successful writer tell me that he never shared tips with other authors about agents or editors because they'd use them to sell their own books. "You have to do it on your own," he said. "If you can't, too bad." Another author is an enemy; they're competition. They're someone who might sell a book when you don't, who might pick up a reader when you don't, who might win a prize when you don't. So, like the TV show *Highlander* (1992–1998), there can be only one—a false narrative. Twenty-five years later, I have many more publications than he does and he no longer publishes. Why? Because I helped others as soon as I had the opportunity, and others helped me. I made great friends, and we helped each other. We shared information, tips, and opportunities. We rose—all together. We knew Epona's wisdom: the herd is stronger than any individual. One horse alone is vulnerable. A herd is unstoppable. If you help each other, you all win. Beli knew this; it is how he defeated the selfish Thunderbolt.

Honor

Another thing Beli knows in the story is honor. Beli is fair and honorable in his dealings with others, while Thunderbolt is underhanded and cruel. Thunderbolt kills Seleucus for gain and murders his sister's children. Ultimately, he is so terrible that even the gods desert him. Our society downplays honor and valorizes cruelty. We think that being honorable means being a chump, a "Boy Scout." Who would you rather have as your king: Beli or Thunderbolt? If we want leaders who behave in admirable ways, we must admire people who behave with honor. That doesn't mean they have to be perfect, squeaky clean, or painfully upright or moralistic and judgmental. But if we admire cruelty, we will get cruelty.

Work

Epona admires hard work. She especially admires the thankless tasks of caring for others and for society that are often overlooked. For example, in a hospital we often think of the surgeons who perform cutting-edge procedures. Epona thinks of the people cleaning the operating theaters, sterilizing everything, laundering the sheets, cooking and delivering the meals, and helping people who can't see change the channels on the TV so they can listen to the news. It's important work without which nothing would happen.

The community needs all kinds of work. The herd needs all members, and its strength is in its cohesion. Whatever your work is or whatever you want it to be, one of the important things is how it benefits the community. Most of us have more than one kind of work. We may have a job and also take care of others or engage in an artistic endeavor. Some of us have more than one job. Some of us volunteer to help the community in a variety of ways. All of these are work.

One flaw the story illuminates in Thunderbolt is his unwillingness to work. He's a prince, and he wants it all because of who he is without working for it. His father decides that he won't be king after him because being king is in fact work! In contrast, Beli is hardworking. He has earned the respect he has due to how he handled his responsibilities.

Epona likes people who are working hard to do things that benefits the community, whether others consider those things important or not. She knows that there is no unimportant job or unimportant member of the herd.

A Rite to Honor Epona

In this rite we will invoke Epona to help in our work. Before you begin, think carefully about what work you want help with. Because her role is Lady of Horses and guardian of the herds, caregiving work is the most appropriate, but any work (paid or unpaid) that benefits the greater community is fine. It should not be something that benefits no one but you. It certainly can be something that only provides financial resources to meet your responsibilities to others, because that is also taking care of them.

When you have thought of the work you want her help with, find a symbol of that work to use. If you like, it can be something wearable—a charm, a pin, a patch, a plastic bracelet for a cause, a part of your work clothing. It can also be something which can go on an altar or desk or somewhere you will see it. If you want to take it with you, it can even be something like a travel mug with a symbol of your work on it. Nobody is going to think that a travel mug with "#1 Nurse" on it is occult! Whatever you choose, make sure it's something you can take to work with you at least occasionally.

This rite is designed for one person alone but can be adapted if you wish to do it with others. If you are doing this with multiple people, each one will need a symbol of their work.

You Will Need

- An image of Epona. If you prefer, you may use an image of a horse.
- The charm or other object you intend to use (if you have more than one person, you will need one each)

- A green or white candle of any size or shape
- Incense and a burner, preferably cedar, pine or another woody scent
- A small pitcher of wine or fruit juice
- A goblet or cup
- A libation bowl

Optional Extras

- A bit of bread and a plate
- A green altar cloth

First, arrange your altar to Epona. Place the image in the center back, and then group the other items pleasingly around it. You may add other embellishments if you wish—more candles, more images, elaborate and fancy dishes to hold the food and drink. It is appropriate to use your best.

Since you are directly petitioning a goddess rather than working a spell or performing a large ritual, you will not need to perform a quarter calling. It is not necessary to call upon deities other than the one you are petitioning.

Prepare by dressing in whatever evokes worship to you, turning off electronic devices or electric lights, and putting yourself in a reflective frame of mind. If you are playing music, you may start the music now.

Light the candle and then the incense if you are using it. Take a moment to center yourself. Say, "Epona, Lady of Horses, guardian and guide, I (we) ask that you attend."

Pour the wine or fruit juice into the goblet. From the goblet, pour a libation into the bowl and then sip from the goblet yourself. Say, "Thank you for sharing this cup with me."

Break the bread and put a piece in the food offerings bowl if you are using bread. Take a taste for yourself as well. Say, "Thank you for sharing this food with me."

Tell Epona in your own words what work you would like her help with. Tell her why it's important to you. Tell her what you do and what challenges you face. As you tell her, perhaps you will think of some specific things that would make your work easier or that would help you to do it. If you do, take this as a cue from her—these are things that would provide real, material help! Focus on concrete things. Epona is a very practical goddess, and she helps with concrete problems. For example, she is not the one to help with a barrier such as a lack of self-confidence. She is the one to help with a problem such as having an impossible schedule or too few resources to do your job. Tell her about concrete problems and listen—you may hear your answer in your question.

When you have finished explaining what it is you need help with, take the tangible symbol of your work that you prepared. Put your fingers on it, tips just touching. Say,

"Epona, Lady of Horses, please help me with practical solutions to my problem. Let this be a symbol of your aid and care as it is a symbol of the work I do. Let me be, as you are, a guardian of the herd. Help me in my work for the benefit of the community so that I can be better at it and better serve those who count on me."

Close your eyes and be still. Try to recapture the peace you felt in the meditation, standing on the green hillside looking at the peacefully grazing herd. Hold that peace. Know that you can reach for it whenever you need it, Epona's touch.

When you feel you are ready, say, "Thank you Epona, for your help and your grace." Blow out the candles and put out the incense if you are using it. Take your offerings outside if you are able to. Finish the portions that were not offered now or soon—do not throw them away.

Take the symbolic object with you and put it where you will see it often. It may be on your altar, in your workspace, or even on a bathroom shelf. It is there to remind you of Epona's help and grace.

In the days that follow, watch for opportunities to make your work better and solve the problems that concern you. Remember that although Epona may be able to give you opportunities, you must speak up for yourself! You may find yourself in a position to express problems to those above you, or to make some changes yourself that will benefit not only you but others who do the same work. Take advantage of those opportunities, knowing that they are given by Epona to those who work for the good of the community. Like Beli in the story, Epona could not fight his battle for him. Beli had to make decisions and fight himself, knowing that Epona's help was his. She will help you, but she will not do the work for you.

Remember too that you may always return to talk to her again. You may find that simply telling her the problems you need help with will help you identify solutions or things that will improve your work. Epona appreciates effort, so even if you are not completely successful or your work is not going well, she understands that you are doing your best. That you strive to make your herds safe is the highest calling as far as she's concerned.

Epona's Correspondences

Here are some correspondences to help you honor Epona, whether it's setting up an altar to her, planning a ritual that invokes her, or simply bringing some of her energy into your daily life.

Colors: Green, white

Incense: Cedar, pine, fir, or another woody scent

Symbols: Horse, dog

Festival Day: June 13

Food: Bread

Chapter Seven

Aphrodite, Queen of the Sea

Aphrodite, the goddess of love, is one of the best-known Hellenistic goddesses. Love has no boundaries, and therefore Aphrodite had none: as Aphrodite Pandemos she was the goddess of all people. In addition, she was also a sea goddess: as Aphrodite Pelagia, she was patron of sailors and fair voyages. Indeed, her worship as a sea goddess seems to pre-date her function as the goddess of love. This story is told as it might have been in the Hellenistic period but is about a time long before, in the Minoan world.

Story: The Sea-Lady's Kingdom

You think she's soft? You think she's a sweet little goddess for lovesick youths to swoon over? Think again. Anyone who makes a life on the sea learns better. Aphrodite Pelagia is nobody's sweet. She may favor you, and if she does, she'll wring you out and lift you up like nothing in this world. If she doesn't, it's the deep, watery grave for you sooner or later. The sea's bright and cold at once, like love. Like her.

The sea walls there, the ones along the harbor that look like they were raised by Titans, the ones that still guard Miletus, were built by those her mercy spared, by the love of the Queen of the Sea.

Long ago, a thousand years and more, there was a city on one of the islands, Thera. There's nothing but a village there now but back then, it was a great city with palaces and harbors and terraced fields and houses perched on the mountain slopes, and every one of them looking out to sea. And at the very top was the palace. And at the very bottom, where you could hear the sea in every room, was the Temple of Aphrodite. They called her by a different name then, but she was the same. She's always the Queen of the Sea.

In that temple was a priestess who served her, and her name was Kassiope. She was a woman of middle years, dark and curving and beautiful, with full breasts over her long skirts that fell in tiers to her feet, and bright eyes that looked on the world with love. She had two children, a girl and a boy. She had two lovers, too. One was Hiero, the ruler of the city, and he was the father of her daughter. The other was Aren, a ship's captain, and he was the father of her son. Both knew of the other, and both could have her and neither keep her, so both were content. Why would they share? Well, one might if one could have a woman like that, priestess of the Queen of the Sea herself, Aphrodite's own handmaiden.

Every morning she would go down the steps to the sea where there was a sheltered pool and she would feed the octopus that lived there. Actually, there was more than one, but they knew her like snakes do in temples now and would come to her and twine around her hands, tasting her skin with their limbs. Sometimes, when it seemed right, one would swim into the pot she carried, curling in the bottom like smoke. On this particular morning Kassiope fed them, and her favorite did this. She lifted the pot up, full of water and the octopus. "There, my friend," she said. And yet for some reason it suddenly took fright, letting off ink and scrambling over the rim to plunge back into the pool, splashing her bright skirts.

Kassiope was ready to exclaim annoyance when the ink caught her. She looked into the depths of the pot, the ink welling up in a column and spreading like a dark blossom. She saw it, the shape of the mountain. She saw the fire and smoke, the landslides rolling down the slopes, the stones and ash falling from the sky to cover all. And beneath her feet she felt what had disturbed the octopus, the faint tremor of the earth awaking.

Now, she knew what a tremor was. The mountain slept. We all know what it feels like when the earth murmurs somewhere down below? Most of the time it's nothing. Sometimes it isn't, and walls fall and stones roll down hills. But this—what she saw in the pot by the Sea Lady's grace, was like nothing she knew. She saw the entire mountain heave, fire going up to the sky, a ring of darkness spreading over the sea, which rose up in waves taller than palaces.

Kassiope dropped the pot and it shattered in fragments on the stone. She stared at it in horror. Surely she had not seen what she thought she saw. And yet beneath her feet there was a faint murmur, far down and soft enough that not even the birds that sheltered on the temple eaves took flight. It couldn't be. She picked up the shards of the pot and threw them away, and she went about her work with a troubled mind.

That night, when her children were sleeping, she went back to the pool in the cool moonlight and walked into the sea, waist deep, the gentle waves splashing against her. "Pelagia," she said, "Sea

Lady, who gives us Your bounty and who hastens our rich trade ships home, is this vision true? And if so, what can I do to save us, Your people who honor You and worship You?"

It was the right question, and the answer came to her as softly as the waves touching her, as soft as the moonlight. "You have ships. They must carry you far from this place. Spread your bright wings and flee as the birds do."

At that she was even more troubled, because how could people be persuaded to do such a thing? The city was rich. There were farms and shops, looms and houses with paintings, goats and dogs and granaries. What could persuade people to leave such a home? It was beautiful beyond compare. She was still thinking the next afternoon when Aren came to her. He had come into port and rushed to see her, a handsome young sailor who loved the sea and who dared every storm and treacherous strait, counting on skill and the love of the Sea Lady. They went to her room and lay together in the sunlight, and when they were done, she cried.

"What is wrong?" Aren asked. "Have I hurt you in some way?" And so Kassiope poured out her vision and what it meant, what the goddess had counseled and how impossible it seemed. Aren listened. His brow knit. "If she says it, it must be true," he said, "for she loves us and it is to her that we owe all our wealth and peace." He turned so that she lay on his breast. "I have seen dead fish floating on the surface of the sea. That only happens when some shock disturbs them far down. I have seen the dolphins swimming away, their pods leaping in the summer air and spray flying as from the prow of a ship. They hear things we do not, deep down beneath the sea."

"They are her creatures," Kassiope said. "If you have seen these portents too, we must go to Hiero."

And so they did, Aren waiting while she walked with Hiero underneath the long portico with its red columns that looked out over the sea. She told him all and then was silent. He did not speak either. She looked at the ocean, and Hiero looked down to the town on the slopes, to houses and markets and port. As they stood, the birds in the trees on the slope below took flight, and then a moment behind they felt the tremor, as though a creature down there in the dark turned over in its sleep, a barely felt rumble far beneath their feet.

Hiero looked at her, and his face was grave. "They will not go," he said, "until it is too late. They won't believe enough to leave this. I'm not sure that I do."

"I do not want to believe," Kassiope said.

He put his hand on her arm. "Go," he said. "Take the children and go with Aren and whoever else will go. I will stay. Maybe it's better to die as I have lived than to lose all I have loved in my life."

She bent her head. "They look to you," she said. "If you do not go, many people will stay because you stay. They will think it is safe." She felt the Sea Queen's hand at her back. "But it will get worse before the end. The tremors will get worse. When they do, people will hear me. Then there must be a plan." She met his eyes. "I will not leave you to die."

She was steel, this woman, implacable as the sea herself, and she would move them all on her shoulders if she needed to. And so she did. She called Aren out and they counted ships and people and animals. It was possible. It could be done to evacuate by sea if people would go. They made a plan.

The tremors grew more frequent, the portents obvious. The birds were gone, flown far away. On the tenth day, the ground

shook in the morning, shifting the temple a little off its founda-
tion, cracking the street where it led into the market, and Kassiope
addressed the crowd that gathered from the temple steps, Aren to
one side and Hiero to the other. She told them plainly what the
Lady of the Sea said and they must leave. Then Hiero stepped forward and said that houses and markets could be rebuilt, but not by
the dead. He ordered by his authority that everyone should evacuate. Even as he spoke, the ground shook again. A small puff of
dark smoke showed at the mountain top.

"It is time!" Kassiope shouted to be heard over the crowd.
"Every person has a place on a ship. We have room for some goods
and animals. There are lists. Come to me or Aren and we will tell
you where your space is waiting for you. The hand of the Sea
Queen lies upon us. She will save us!"

Now you might think that people panicked, but they didn't.
They can be remarkably calm in a disaster if there's a good
example. There was, and they loved Hiero, and they followed.
Yes, in the end every last person followed. Not one remained in
the town, nor one dog or goat. It took two days embarking, and
the ships set off as they did, one by one. Where did they go, you
ask? Here is where they came, Miletus behind its headland. There
was a fishing village here and good harbor, but most importantly
there was the headland, a strip of land with cliffs forty feet high
that sheltered the harbor behind it.

The last ship was Aren's. Kassiope was with him, having sent
the children with Hiero on a ship three hours earlier. They were
well out to sea, looking back at the mountain when it blew. A column of fire rose to the sky and rivers of molten stone ran down its
slopes. Ash came down like rain.

Kassiope stood in horror but Aren shouted aloud. "Rowers!" he yelled, "Bring us about! Put our prow into it!" He saw the wave. It rose, high as houses, a vast green shape like a monster rising from the deeps, foam-crowned. It was three times the length of the ship.

The rowers put their backs to it, and Aren had the tiller himself, turning, turning as the wave came on. Would it catch them broadside, tipping them and throwing them like a leaf in a fast moving stream? It rose above them just as they turned.

The ship mounted its face, prow breaking through the crest with a wash of water down the sides, white spray flying, and then they were down the backside of it. Pumice floated on the sea.

"Come about again!" Aren shouted, "Follow it!" because of course he was afraid of what might have happened to the rest of the fleet ahead. And indeed, one ship was capsized and some lost, but most of the ships weathered the great wave. The wave crashed into the headland, spray mounting above it, but the harbor behind was safe, and here they came to rest. Aren ran the ship in and Kassiope leaped over the rail, running to grab her children who came to meet her, kneeling with them in the lapping surf. Hiero and Aren looked back, the vast column of smoke over the sea rising to the heavens like ripples in the pool of the sky.

The land was lost but the people saved and they tell its story still: the Sea Lady's kingdom in all its beauty and its fiery end, and how she saved those who trusted in her. So next time you think she's soft, think of this. Aphrodite is no weak thing. They were saved by love of each other.

Questions to Consider

Now that you have read a story about Aphrodite, take out your journaling materials, either paper and a writing implement or an electronic means of journaling. It's time to consider your reaction to the story you just read.

- What is your immediate, emotional reaction to Aphrodite's story?

- How many different kinds of relationships and kinds of love do you see in the story? How does each love contribute to the ending? Did any of them surprise you?

- What did you think of Aphrodite's indirect hand in this?

- How does this story surprise you? Is it different from your previous picture of Aphrodite? Would you feel comfortable invoking her? Why or why not?

Ancient Worship: Aphrodite

The eruption of the volcanic island of Thera is a real event that happened in the sixteenth century BCE. At that time the island was home to an amazing Minoan city now known as Akrotiri. It was a wealthy trading port that had broad streets and terraced multistory houses. Amazingly, despite the eruption and being buried in ash, not one set of human or animal remains have been found, and very few small valuables. There are enormous pots four feet tall, large pieces of furniture and the like, but it is clear to archaeologists that the city was evacuated in an orderly fashion before the eruption. What an amazing feat! Imagine knowing that the eruption was imminent without geologists or seismologists. Imagine evacuating a city without loss of life—hard enough to do today, and yet they did. This is a story of how that might have happened.

The houses were decorated with beautiful wall paintings, many of which have endured in amazing, vibrant color. Since Akrotiri was discovered, people have hypothesized that this was the origin of the ancient story of the lost city of Atlantis. The Minoan civilization on Thera does fit the descriptions that Plato provides beautifully, including that it was on the slopes of a volcano and was destroyed by the eruption.[27] Pottery from the site places it in the right time period, the sixteenth century BCE. Because Akrotiri was evacuated, there were clearly survivors who could spread the story and who presumably settled in other places where their advanced Minoan civilization was remarkable.

Aphrodite herself was said to have been born only about sixty miles away, on the island of Cythera. Certainly the area was an early center of her worship. Temples and rites to Aphrodite Pelagia abounded in port cities in the Aegean and particularly on Cyprus in the Eastern Mediterranean.

Meeting Aphrodite: A Meditation

This meditation may be done in two different ways: Find a partner to read it to you and take turns doing the meditation, or simply read it in a quiet place or even record it and play it to yourself.

You will need a quiet place where you won't be disturbed for twenty minutes or so. You may play soft music if you like. If you have music you normally use while meditating, you may certainly use it. If you would like to use incense, consider one of the recommendations in the correspondences section at the end of this chapter.

This may be an intense experience. Read through the meditation before you begin and decide if it is something you want to do.

---

27. Patricia Claus, "New Findings on Santorini Point to Lost Island of Atlantis Origins" *The Greek Reporter*, May 2021, https://greekreporter.com /2021/05/21/new-findings-on-santorini-point-to-lost-island-of -atlantis-origins/.

Take a deep breath to help you relax. Then take another. Now begin either reading to yourself or listening as the meditation is read to you. If you are having it read to you, close your eyes. Otherwise, read aloud slowly so that you have time to absorb the words.

You are walking on the beach at night. It's beautiful and peaceful, a full moon over the ocean making a path across the waves. The seas are gentle, little waves flowing in from a calm sea, breaking almost on the shore and lapping at the sand. You stroll along the edge of the waves, letting them wash over your feet from time to time, your toes digging deep into the cool sand. There is no sound except the breeze and the waves, soothing and calm. The moonlight makes a path across the water.

You walk for some distance, but you aren't tired. It's so refreshing, so calming. You see a woman ahead. She's coming toward you, the ocean kissing her feet. She's nude, the most beautiful woman you've ever seen, completely unselfconscious and relaxed. Her smile is brighter than the stars as she sees you, as though she is utterly delighted to greet you. You can't help but smile back. Her expression awakens joy.

You know that this is Aphrodite, the Queen of the Seas herself. Take a moment to look at her. Her beauty is whatever you consider most beautiful; she has had many faces through the ages, and tastes in beauty are intensely personal. As you think this, her smile widens. "If everyone in the world wanted the same woman, where would we be? Everyone is desirable to the right person, just as everyone is beautiful. You are beautiful."

She means it. That may be difficult to believe, or it may be very easy, but her eyes are sincere. You know she's speaking the truth.

"Walk with me," she says, "on this beautiful night." You walk down the beach beside her. She walks on the water side, the waves lapping higher on her than you, the soft sound of the ocean surrounding you. "Tell me about your loves," she says. "Tell me about the people you love most in the world."

You think for a moment. Who do you love? Who is at the center of your heart? It may be a lover or partner, parent or child, dear friend or sibling. Tell her about the people you love, all of them, in their variety.

Aphrodite listens. She hears the words of your heart. She understands love in all its forms, no matter how usual or unusual it is. However you experience love, it is not new to her. It is part of her experience, part of her realm, just like the mighty seas which are calm for you here and now.

She catches that thought. "Love," she says, "can be wild and dangerous. It is always difficult to give your heart. It's always risky. Other people are not in your control, and they may always do things that hurt you. The seas are unpredictable. And yet that is where life is—out in the great depths, in the teeming shallows, in the green waters. You are meant for love."

Her words strike deep. You are meant for love.

Aphrodite smiles. "You are meant for love like a porpoise for the waves. You have what you need to swim these waters. Everything you need to navigate the currents of the heart is already inside you, here." She touches your chest lightly, just above your heart. "Simply love."

It gives you a sense of peace. You have what you need. Even if it's hard to identify at the moment, it's there.

Or perhaps it's easy. Perhaps your loves are returned and you are very happy in them. If so, you know that she is right. You have what you need.

Aphrodite takes a step back. "Go on, sweetheart," she says. "I'll be right here if you need me." She turns and starts walking down the beach away from you, the waves playing around her ankles, washing in and then receding.

You take a long moment to breathe in the peace of the moment, the long moment of quiet when she leaves you, like the breath after love. Then you start walking in the opposite direction.

You walk back into your life, into the world that you left.

Take a moment to ground and center and come back fully. When you are ready, turn off the music or ocean sounds if you are using them, and put out any incense or candles. Take a deep breath and thank the goddess for her attention.

Lessons from Aphrodite: Goddess of Love

Now that you've read a story about Aphrodite and done a meditation to meet her, let's talk a little bit about her gifts.

Shades of Love

In the story, we saw examples of different kinds of love: Kassiope's love for both Hiero and Aren and their love for her; her love for her children and presumably Hiero's love too, since he took them to safety; Aren's love for the sea; Hiero's love for Akrotiri; Kassiope's love for the goddess she served. And there was the love of the Lady of the Sea for all of these people. We are often used to thinking of love, especially of Aphrodite, in the sense of purely romantic or sexual love, however that was the province of Eros, Aphrodite's son. The Goddess of Love, Aphrodite Pandemos, is the goddess of all kinds of love. Romantic and sexual love is part of that, but only part.

All of these kinds of love made escape from the erupting volcano possible. Kassiope loved Aren and trusted his observations of sea creatures that confirmed her vision. Hiero loved Kassiope and believed her when she said that an eruption was imminent. All of them were spurred to action by love for their children. Aren's love of the sea and the skill he had gained as a sailor made it possible to survive the tidal wave through his quick and correct actions. Hiero's love of Akrotiri made it imperative to him to save everyone who lived there. And most of all, Kassiope's love of the Lady of the Sea and her service to her goddess brought her the warning in the first place. Romantic and sexual love, love of family, love of one's work, love of others, and love of the gods are all shades of love.

How do you experience these loves in your life? Are any of them uncomfortable? In your opinion, are any of them less important or valid? Are any related to things you wish you had positive experiences with but don't? Many people have scars or bad experiences that taint how they see some kinds of love. For example, if you grew up in a toxic religious environment, you may see love of the gods as a frightening or unattainable thing. Perhaps you were raised not to value one kind of love or taught that certain relationships were not important. Or perhaps because of past relationships, you see love of family as dangerous or unnecessary. After a bad experience with a kind of love, it's easy to dismiss it or devalue it in others. It's easy to close a wounded heart. Aphrodite understands that. She knows that not everyone is able to experience every kind of love, especially if they have been hurt.

She extends her hands to heal hearts in time. Continuing the previous example, if you are too close to a toxic religious upbringing to experience the love of the gods, that doesn't mean you always will be. Time passes. Hearts heal with Aphrodite's help. She understands the mutability of feeling. We try to put ourselves in little boxes and define ourselves and others. And yet feelings change. We grow. We put out branches in a new direction. How we feel today may not be how we feel in twenty years. We must allow for the growth of the heart. We must give ourselves room for healing and change. To be "open-hearted" is to be ready to let love in, in whatever form it takes.

Trust

Another thing we saw in the story was trust, which is born out of love. Over and over, people trusted one another and trusted in the Lady of the Sea. That trust was what allowed them to survive. However, when society or relationships are damaged, the first thing that falls is trust. Without it, it's difficult for people to function together. We live in a time when trust in others is easily eroded. One has only to look at social media to see a torrent of cruelty and disrespect. We may not be experiencing a catastrophic volcanic eruption, but we have experienced catastrophes in our lives. How have they damaged our trust for others? How have they rebuilt it? One of the most harmful secondary effects of catastrophe has been isolating people from the social ties and relationships that make them happy. One of the things we might ask Aphrodite for is help in rebuilding those ties. Like the people of Akrotiri, we need to live in a whole and complete society where we can trust one another. It is entirely appropriate to ask her to help us heal hearts and rebuild relationships that depend on trust.

As individuals, we need to have people we count on. To do that, we need to be trustworthy. Think about you have built trust with. Who trusts you because you have been there for them? How has that helped your relationship grow and deepen? Trust is an important component of love; it's one of the things that helps it endure.

Faith

Faith is an outgrowth of trust. Faith is knowing that someone will behave in a certain way when you have no way to control it or know what is happening. For example, if your mother always picks you up at a certain time, you have faith that she will arrive today unless some unfortunate event prevents her. You don't have to check up on her. If you have a monogamous relationship or a relationship where you ask one another about outside relationships, knowing your partner is faithful means you know they will not sleep with a random person they meet tomorrow. You don't have to examine their phone or have someone follow them around if they're not with you. Likewise, if your best friend has always been honest with you, you can have faith in what they tell you. Faith in the gods is simply an extension of this. If you have a relationship that you know is solid, you can rely on it.

In the story, Kassiope has a relationship with Aphrodite Pelagia rooted in faith. She knows the Lady of the Sea has her back and would never give her frivolous advice or lead her astray. She knows that the warning she receives is real and in fact wishes it weren't. Kassiope's reluctance to believe is not because she doesn't trust the Lady of the Sea but because she doesn't want to believe that this terrible thing is going to happen. It's understandable and common to react to bad news with denial at first.

Faith is a hard word for many of us. It may suggest blind or irrational belief in things that don't feel right, but that's not faith. Faith is based on a relationship. It comes after the relationship, not before. It grows from love and trust. "Have faith" is a useless direction, like "fall in love." If the ingredients of the relationship aren't there first, it can't be done. Kassiope's faith is based on a relationship of many years with her goddess in the same way that people who have been together a long time have faith in each other to follow the rules of their relationship without checking on each other. Whether a person or a god, think about who you have faith in and how that love and trust developed. One of Aphrodite's gifts is the deep love that grows over time.

A Rite to Honor Aphrodite

In this rite we will invoke Aphrodite to help in our relationships. Before you begin, think carefully about what relationship you want help with. It does not have to be a romantic relationship, but it does have to be a loving and personal one. It may be with a romantic partner, or a parent, child, or someone you love as a sibling. It does not have to be a bad relationship or one that troubles you. Perhaps the relationship is extremely happy and you would like it to remain a source of strength and joy to you as the world throws crisis after crisis at you! Remember in the story what enabled everyone to work together with trust and purpose was the golden thread of Kassiope's relationships.

This rite is designed for one person alone but can be adapted if you wish to do it with others. If you are doing this with multiple people, each one will need a symbol of their relationship.

You Will Need

- An image of Aphrodite. These are easy to find and there are many beautiful images on the internet that you can print out and use if you do not have one already.

- A seashell or a charm in the shape of a seashell if you wish to wear it (if you have more than one person, you will need one for each of you)

- A blue candle of any size and shape

- Incense and a burner, preferably rose or jasmine or another rich floral scent

- A small pitcher of wine or fruit juice

- A goblet or cup

- A libation bowl

Optional Extras

- A plate of honey cakes such as baklava

- A blue altar cloth

- Additional seashells for decoration

- Seashell shaped dishes, candle-holders, or whatever else invokes the Lady of the Sea to you

- Music that invokes the ocean or the sound of ocean waves and a way to play it

First, arrange your altar to Aphrodite. Place the image in the center back, and then group the other items pleasingly around it. You may add other embellishments if you wish—more candles, more images, elaborate and fancy dishes to hold the food and drink. You may add seashells or sea-themed decorations as you want. It is appropriate to use your best.

Since you are directly petitioning a goddess rather than working a spell or performing a large ritual, you will not need to perform a quarter calling. It is not necessary to call upon deities other than the one you are petitioning.

Prepare by dressing in whatever evokes worship to you, turning off electronic devices or electric lights, and putting yourself in a reflective frame of mind. If you plan on using music or ocean wave sounds, play them now.

Light the candle and the incense if you are using it. Take a moment to center yourself. Say, "Aphrodite, Queen of the Seas, Lady of Love, I (we) ask that you attend."

Pour the wine or fruit juice into the goblet. Pour a libation into the bowl and then sip from the goblet yourself. Say, "Thank you for sharing this cup with me."

Break or cut a honey cake if you are using them. Place one piece in the offering plate and eat another, savoring the sweetness of the honey. Say, "Thank you for sharing with me the sweetness of life."

Tell Aphrodite in your own words about the person you love. Tell her why they are wonderful and what it is that you so love and cherish about them. Don't be shy—explain at length exactly why this person is special to you. If more than one person is doing the rite, let each person have a chance to share their love. There is a reason this needs to be spoken aloud: this is a declaration of love, like a proposal. It's not secret. It's not hidden. This is shouting your love to the heavens, proclaiming it to the Queen of the Sea! In some of Aphrodite's temples were votive offerings, statues or such that were given to her and often inscribed with the name of the person the giver loved, e.g., "For my wife, Selene." You are speaking aloud your love.

When you have expressed your love, ask Aphrodite for whatever help you wish: "I wish that our relationship could continue for the rest of our lives." "I hope that my relationship with my son will improve and that he will appreciate the support of his family." "I ask for your help in mending my relationship with my best friend, because our argument was stupid compared to all the times we've been there for each other."

Your request should not contain blame or manipulation—Aphrodite doesn't like those behaviors, and she especially doesn't like deceptive lovers. She will not help you lie to someone. Also, this is not the time to try to get back at someone; she takes a dim view of that. You are trying to improve a relationship or continue it, not change someone in it. If you say something like, "I want our relationship to improve by them deciding that they want what I want," that isn't going to fly. Aphrodite will do what is best for both of you, and if it's not positive for them as well as for you, she won't help. Remember, love and trust must be a two-way street. If the other person does not love and trust you or desire a relationship with you, Aphrodite is not going to help you attain it.

Pick up the charm or seashell you have chosen. Say, "Aphrodite, Queen of the Seas, please let this serve as a token of my love, blessed by you." If multiple people are performing this rite, each person should do this. Then take the charm or shell and wear it or put it somewhere on you. You may keep it or wear it as long as you like for as long as you feel that it is still meaningful to you.

Close your eyes and try to recapture the peace you felt in the meditation, standing on the beach with Aphrodite. Listen to the sound of the waves. If you are using recorded ocean sounds, this is easy. If not, simply imagine the sound of the ocean.

When you feel you are ready, say, "Thank you Aphrodite, for your love and your peace." Blow out the candles and put out the incense if you are using it. Take your offerings outside if you are able. Finish the portions that were not offered now or soon but do not throw them away. It is especially good to share the honey cakes with others whom you care for.

In the days that follow, look for opportunities to be loving. Look for moments when you can express love for others, whether with the person you wanted to improve your relationship with or someone else entirely. It may be that you have the opportunity to show your love for someone close to you. It may be that a stranger needs someone to acknowledge them and care about them in some small way. However the moments come, act with love, as though each action was a gift to Aphrodite. Bear in mind the Sea Queen's gifts to you, the strength of love.

Aphrodite's Correspondences

Here are some correspondences to help you honor Aphrodite, whether it's setting up an altar to her, planning a ritual that invokes her, or simply bringing some of her energy into your daily life.

Colors: Blue, pink, emerald, copper

Incense: Rose, jasmine

Symbols: Seashells, roses, flowers, pearls

Festival Day: May 1 or the full moon of May

Food: Seafood, honey cakes

Chapter Eight

Cybele, Death and Rebirth

It's hard to imagine the controversies that raged around the worship of this ancient goddess, but the worship of Cybele was one of the most contentious in the Hellenistic world. Invited by some states and banned in others, her priests, the *galli*, were both revered and reviled. Death and rebirth are always scary subjects, but because Cybele's priests were considered neither men nor women, her worship was especially frightening to some cultures. Parts of the Hellenistic world had a long history of accepting a third gender, while others emphatically did not. To assign that gender a liminal role, standing between death and rebirth in such a position of power, seemed to challenge any number of cultures. The Romans especially were both intrigued and dismayed by Cybele's worship, both inviting it into the city of Rome and then trying to limit and regulate it.

This story invites you to imagine that you are a Roman traveler who has come to the Hellenistic city of Pergamon hoping to learn more of Cybele's mysteries than are available to you in Rome.

Story: A Young Man's Death

You've come a long way to die, young man. Pergamon is far from Rome. It may as well be in the uttermost east, as far as Romans are concerned. Not quite off the map, but nearly so. And yet you came, of course, for Cybele. In Her name I welcome you.

I know why you came. You were going about your staid life, a model young citizen, and yet somehow dissatisfied. How could you be? You were a Roman citizen, surely the highest creature on earth. And yet something was wrong, something indefinable, something you could not even name. Was it Her touch? Was there something you did not find in your tame gods? Oh yes, I know the Roman Senate welcomed Cybele when they thought She would help them against the Carthaginians, but they bound Her, did they not? Her priests were restricted to their temple except for feast-days, Her worship constrained by their rules. They thought they could tame Her, that being in Rome She would become Roman. They were wrong.

She was born here, in the forests of Asia Minor, long ago before even the Hittites ruled. Sometimes we find Her image in a dark cave, the carving of a woman no bigger than our hands, Her breasts and Her hips broad and full, put down there in the dark for worship in a place which is like a tomb. She was here long before ships plied the seas. She was here long before cities were raised. When the bright sea people and their sea-born goddess came, she was already here, deep in the pine woods beneath the mountain peaks, in caves that wind down into the dark. Cybele is older than mountains.

Was it the tambours that woke something in your soul? Did you stop on the street, confounded, when one of Her processions passed by? A few times a year, they are loosed from the bounds, Her galli, Her priests, Her sons, Her lovers. Did you see them passing? They danced as they walked, long, bleached hair flowing, robed like priestesses with garlands, eyes lined with kohl, bare feet ornamented with ankle bracelets. They danced as they walked, striking their tambours and cymbals, striking fear into the hearts of those who watched, so fierce and unfamiliar, so wild and fabulous. Did you watch, young man? Did you yearn?

No Roman citizen can join them. It is prohibited by law. And yet.

Did you hear the story, garbled and transformed? Attis was Her son. No, he was Her lover. He was unfaithful. He was attacked. He was penitent. There are different versions, but they all lead to the same thing: he was castrated. He was no longer a man. He was something else, something in between, someone neither male nor female. He was a gallus. And he was Her love, Her life, Her breath, and reborn in Her.

Or is it that She was his life, his breath? Was it that he was put in a tomb and raised from the dead to be at Her side, reborn in the blood of the bull? Or was he reborn in his own blood, in the blood that flowed where his testicles were removed, the bloody scraps of his former life which were flung on the housetop in challenge or mourning or triumph?

You blanch, but you do not move. You have come to die.

Oh yes, you can still leave. But you won't. Not if you have come so far. Not if you have named what you want. You will die. The young man who came here will go into the tomb. Your blood will be shed. You will lie in pain and rise in joy. You will be that man no longer. You will have a new name. He will be dead. You will be someone else. You will be Attis. You will be a gallus.

Your kin will mourn you. They will not recognize you if they see you, and probably they never will. They will say you died in the East.

And you—you will be Hers. You will live as you wish to, fierce and furious and free, betwixt and between, neither and both. Perhaps you will stay here. Perhaps you will journey Her pine forests and mountains. Perhaps you will go to the cities of the coast, dancing in the streets of Tyre or Biruta or Ashkelon. Perhaps you will tend a temple or lead in song. Perhaps you will speak truth to rulers who rightly listen when the dance comes to their door, pouring out gold into the hands of Her dancers, the wild throng whose death and rebirth renews the earth. There are many such in lands far from Rome.

You have come here to die so that you can live. Be welcome in Cybele's grace.

Questions to Consider

Now that you have read a story about Cybele, take out your journaling materials, either paper and a writing implement or an electronic means of journaling. It's time to consider your reaction to the story you just read.

- What is your immediate, emotional reaction to the story?
- Are there things that shock or surprise you? Is that in a positive or negative way?
- Cybele and worship of her were controversial in Rome but much less so in the Hellenistic world, where it was

widespread. Why do you think this was? Do you think her worship would be controversial today?

- How does Cybele's worship speak to you or not? What do you think of her role as ancient earth goddess? Of her role as patron of the galli?

Ancient Worship: Cybele

Cybele may have origins as the great earth mother of Anatolia. Representations of a voluptuous female figure go back to the stone age, as they do in other parts of the world. She is also shown seated with animals on either side of her throne, perhaps symbolizing the domestication of animals before agriculture.[28]

Deep Earth Mother

Later representations show Cybele flanked by lions, an indication of her connection to the wild rather than the settled lives of farms and cities. As such, she is revered and feared at the same time—the wild is necessary but seems frightening to those who are unfamiliar with it. Cybele is the goddess of deep places, the impenetrable wilderness, the caves that go down into strange worlds of darkness. Not the underworld—the wild.

She is also the guardian of those deep and dark places in ourselves, the welling springs far underground that never see light. She is the foster-mother of Dionysus, the god of the vine whose revelry brings renewal, but whose madness is awful indeed. She is associated with Pan, the god of the forests and mountains, who likewise cannot be controlled. Associated with Rhea, she is the fertility of the earth

---

28. keegan1234, "Cybele, the Mother Goddess," *Women in Antiquity* (blog), November 2018, https://womeninantiquity.wordpress.com/2018/11/27/cybele-the-mother-goddess/.

far from plowed fields, far from lands tamed by humans to grow things that are useful to them. She watches over the liminal spaces between the civil and the untamed.[29]

Cybele's worship spread across the Hellenistic world from the fourth century BCE, with notable sites in the Kingdom of Pergamon and in the coastal cities of the eastern Mediterranean. From Pergamon it spread to Rome. According to the Roman historian Livy, Cybele was "invited" to Rome in 204 BCE because of a prophecy. She arrived in the form of a black stone brought from Asia Minor which was then housed in a temple built for her.[30]

However, in Rome and then in the areas conquered by Rome, which included much of the Hellenistic World, Cybele's worship was tightly constrained. Her priests, the galli, were prohibited from leaving the temple enclave except at certain times under certain circumstances, notably on Cybele's feast days to participate in her rites. Nevertheless, her worship spread. Indeed, the grave of a gallus has been discovered as far away as Britain, in Yorkshire![31]

Panic (or Pan-ic)

What was the reason for these restrictions in Rome and under Roman rule when they did not exist in the Hellenistic world? The answer may be the ancient equivalent of trans panic.

In the Hellenistic world, the roles of women were much broader than in Rome, certainly in the second and third centuries BCE when Cybele's worship came to Rome. For example, we have

---

29. Robert Turcan, *The Cults of the Roman Empire* (London: Blackwell Publishers, 1996), 28–30.

30. Ibid., 36–37.

31. "Dig Reveals Roman Transvesite" BBC News, May 21, 2002 http://news.bbc .co.uk/2/hi/uk_news/england/1999734.stm.

ample evidence of women holding important civic jobs themselves, including being elected to offices, not as wives or daughters. There are numerous inscriptions that refer to women as magistrates, elected judges.[32] This was absolutely not the case in Rome. To call a Roman man "womanly" or "feminine" was a deadly insult. What could be more of a challenge to Roman manhood than a man who wanted to be a woman? What could be more appalling, more provoking of diatribes about "Eastern barbarians" than the idea of castration, of a man physically altering his body to no longer be a man?

In much of the eastern Mediterranean there was a long tradition of a third gender, the eunuch, who was genetically male but had been castrated and thus was neither male nor female. While some eunuchs were slaves and were castrated involuntarily, the eunuchs who served various gods were generally people who had chosen it and had sought a social role that would allow them to live as a third gender. That Cybele's priests were nonbinary was no shock to people in much of the Hellenistic world, but it was a cause of panic in Rome. Or is it Pan-ic?

The original meaning of the word "panic" meant to be filled with the madness of Pan, to be transported by wildness, lifted out of an ordinary state of mind and moved by ecstatic madness. Imagine the reaction of staid citizens to the procession of Cybele! Her galli marched through the streets with tambourines and flutes, dancing as they went. Their long hair was bleached. They wore ankle bracelets with little bells. They wore what were considered at the time women's clothes and makeup. They were

32. Ross Kraemer, ed., *Maenads, Martyrs, Matrons and Monastics: A Sourcebook on Women's Religions in the Greco-Roman World* (Philadelphia: Fortress Press, 1988), 216–217.

furious and fabulous. Doesn't this remind you of Stonewall, when drag queens led the way in the battle for LGBTQ+ rights? Doesn't this divine chaos, the upending of society, the challenge to conventional views of gender and shame and limitation with the glorious beauty of unconformity, seem quite familiar? If you've been to a Pride parade, you may have felt something like what people felt when the galli led the sacred processions of Cybele.

Loss and Renewal

Cybele is also the goddess of death and rebirth, of loss and renewal. Each year, her beloved Attis dies. Each year he is the sacrifice, and each year he returns. Her major rites were held at the spring equinox, around early March to mid-April depending on location, and there is an obvious connection to the return to fertility of the earth. Attis is killed, his blood spread on the ground, and from it grows this year's crop. Alternately, he is castrated, and from his testicles arises new growth. Cybele fulfills both roles: the mourning mother or lover left behind and the dark goddess beneath the earth who receives him and assists in his rebirth.

In addition is the less literal meaning, that in order to grow we must experience loss. We cannot start over without losing what we had before. The galli lived this story. In order to become a new person with a new name, the person they had been before had to ritually die. Just as today many trans people refer to their previous identity as their "dead name," so the galli left behind their previous identities when they "died." The story at the beginning of the chapter mentioned this in the journey of a young Roman man who left his home and went to Pergamon so that he could die and be reborn in Cybele's service.

The cycle of death and rebirth doesn't just apply to gender, however. Loss and renewal are part of life. We may end a relationship and experience the loss that encompasses, yet without that loss we cannot start over with someone else. We end one job and say farewell to something that has been important to us so that we can begin something different. We move from one home to another. We say goodbye to adult children moving out as we begin a new part of our own lives. Throughout our lives we transition from one state to another. Death and rebirth, loss and renewal, is part of being human. Cybele rules over these transitions.

Meeting Cybele: A Meditation

Now that we have read a story about Cybele and learned a little more about her, let's meet her with a meditation. This meditation may be done in two different ways: Find a partner to read it to you and take turns doing the meditation, or simply read it in a quiet place or even record it and play it to yourself.

You will need a quiet place where you won't be disturbed for twenty minutes or so. You may play soft music if you like. If you have music you normally use while meditating, you may certainly use it. If you would like to use incense, consider one of the recommendations in the correspondences section at the end of this chapter.

Take a deep breath to help you relax. Then take another. Now begin either reading to yourself or listening as the meditation is read to you. If you are having it read to you, close your eyes. Otherwise, read aloud slowly so that you have time to absorb the words.

This may be an intense experience. Read through the meditation before you begin and decide if it is something you want to do.

You are walking in a forest at night. All around you enormous pine trees reach toward the starry sky. Their branches sway in a light wind, a whisper of needles as branches touch one another. Beneath the trees, all is peaceful. You are walking on a carpet of pine needles, your feet soundless. You meander through the trees, always going up as the path seems to lead higher.

After a little bit, you come to a steeper slope, but you climb it effortlessly, going up a path. Now and again you see through the trees that there is a drop-off to one side. You are on a mountain, climbing up the side of a great peak, but your course between the trees is still easy. You can sometimes hear the sound of running water, as if a stream paralleled you further down. It's very peaceful. Take a moment to smell the pine sap and listen to the life of the forest.

And yet beneath the scent of the forest is the smell of a campfire. You look around. Higher up the mountain there is a wink of light, red amid the trees. Someone is there. Someone is waiting for you.

You walk between the great trees and make your way toward the fire. At last you step into a clearing. The stars are very bright above. The trees seem to bend toward the center. A black stone rests dug deep into the earth, as though long ago a meteor fell, its core embedding itself in this clearing. Before it, a fire blazes in a black brazier. Behind it stands a woman.

She is fifty or sixty, with a proud, defiant face. She looks at you over the stone, and you bow to her. "Why have you sought me?" Cybele asks. "Why have you come to this wild place? What are you looking for?"

You tell her in your own words. Do you seek wisdom? Solace? Renewal? Comfort? Or is it simply curiosity that brings you here? You tell her the reasons and she nods slowly.

"You stand at the gates of mystery," she says. "In the outermost chambers of the depths. If you wish to go further, you must walk a longer path."

You know this. You have not come here to be initiated. You have come here to meet her. "Mighty One, I do not seek initiation at this time," you say. "I merely wish to learn and share with you these offerings."

"That is pleasing," she says. "For my heart is deep as wilderness, and the way is perilous. I will accept your offerings and welcome you. You may use this place to renew your spirit, and if you wish to go deeper, you must seek me and say so."

"Thank you, Mighty One," you say. You glance away, toward the sound of running water, and when you look back she is gone. You are alone in the clearing before the stone, the fires lighting the night. All around you is the profound peace of the forest. The trees shift in the breeze, the firelight flickering. You pause, simply breathing in the quiet. You know there are mysteries beyond, but for now you may simply rest.

When you are ready, you begin to walk back down the path. It leads you beneath the mighty branches, along the descending path, until you reach the glade where you began. Then the forest begins to fade around you, the trees becoming transparent and indistinct as you return to ordinary life.

Take a moment to ground and center and come back fully. When you are ready, turn off the music or forest sounds and to put out any incense or candles. Take a deep breath and thank Cybele for her attention.

Think for a moment about your experience. What did it feel like? How do you feel now?

Lessons from Cybele: Cybele's Gifts

Now that you've read a story about Cybele and done a meditation to meet her, let's talk a little bit about her gifts.

The Wild Inside

Have you ever felt that there was something fierce inside you like a tiger or bird of prey just waiting to break free? Have you ever dreamed of falling from a great height and then spreading your wings and soaring like a bird? Have you ever felt the swoop of freedom driving on a long, empty highway when it seems there's nothing between you and the horizon? You have felt the wild inside.

Maybe you've experienced it in music, at a concert or playing for an audience. Maybe you've felt it on the dance floor, transformed by the beat. Maybe you've felt it alone, journeying in the wilderness where the sky seems so big. There is something inside you that is furious, fierce, fabulous, and strange in its beauty—this is the part that Cybele's mysteries speak to.

Like most of us today, most people in the Hellenistic world lived lives circumscribed by civilization. We are parts of communities, families, and peer groups. We are responsible. We can't just take off in the car and drive to the horizon, even if sometimes there is a part of us that wants to. And yet sometimes we must touch that part, that renewing and cleansing joy and madness that opens us up to possibility. In many cities in the Hellenistic world, there was a space for that freedom. The annual festival in honor of Cybele around the spring equinox gave people a chance to let go, be outside the rules, follow the dancers, and be transformed. It may be that today's Mardi Gras and Carnival celebrations are the distant descendants of this Cybele's festival: participants wear masks and can put on other identities, putting aside the responsibilities of everyday life. Sometimes we all need to do this. A vacation where we can act differently from our usual or a club or party—sometimes we all need to touch the wild inside.

Transformation

Perhaps the greatest of Cybele's gifts is transformation. Sometimes it's not just that we need a break from our lives, we need to change them. We need to permanently change ourselves. Perhaps we're facing the end of a relationship or the beginning of one. Perhaps we are going to move across the country, go back to school, live in a place entirely different from anywhere we've lived, or do something that feels dangerous. We need to make a hard transition so that we can become something new. The galli, like modern transgender people, were literally leaving their old lives behind. Maybe it's as sharp as that.

One of Cybele's gifts is to guide us through hard transitions, the death of the old and the birth of the new. As such, her mysteries are profound and deep beyond the scope of this book. Perhaps what we need to know here is that at some point in our lives, we are all transformed. None of us remain who we were at the age of twelve for our whole lives. Maybe we undergo transformation at twenty. Or at forty or sixty. Maybe we transform more than once. But we all change, and giving space to that is one of the most critical things we can do. Today, there's often the rejection of the idea that personal evolution is natural. After all, don't we have immutable identity? But of course we don't. We change our understanding of ourselves throughout our lives as we grow. The only way to not evolve is never to grow; imagine being seventy years old as an over-grown eighteen-year-old who never learned anything from life's experiences.

Sometimes our identity changes. We choose a new title: director, doctor, or dad. We identify with a different religious group or political party. We may change how we identify our gender or our heritage. These are major transformations. Cybele's gifts help us shed our old skin and become comfortable in our new one.

A Rite to Honor Cybele

Now that we have learned more about Cybele, we are going to ask for her assistance with some transition in our lives. The last few years have been difficult; many of us have lost something important to us, be it a person who has died or left our lives, or our life circumstances themselves have changed. Maybe we've had to rethink cherished plans or let go of a future we hoped for. Maybe we've decided to do something different but still mourn the past. It's okay for transitions to be hard. It's okay to feel a sense of loss. Cybele is there to help us navigate this.

Before you begin, think of something that you are ready and willing to let go of. Do not choose things that you feel uncomfortable letting go. Asking for her help with renewal only works if you truly consent to it in your heart. For example, if people in your life are telling you to move past a relationship and you don't feel it is time yet, you're not done. Do not bury a part of you that lives. Choose something where you are indeed ready for renewal.

This rite is designed for one person alone but can be adapted if you wish to do it with others. It may be intense, so consider who you want to share this with. This rite also involves dance and movement but neither needs to be any particular kind or at a particular level of energy. Anyone can do this as they are able, whether as seated movement or with limited mobility. Dance does not have to be vigorous standing movement. The amount of movement you incorporate is entirely up to you.

You Will Need

- An image of Cybele. If you do not have one, find one on the internet and print it out.
- A pinecone or pinecones
- A dark green or black candle of any size or shape you like
- Incense and a burner, preferably pine, fir, or cedar
- A small pitcher of wine or fruit juice
- A goblet or cup
- A libation bowl
- Any music that makes you want to dance plus a way to play it

Optional Extras

- Nuts, nut bread, or mushrooms
- A plate for food offerings if you are using them
- A dark green or black altar cloth
- Tambourines, bells, or hand cymbals

First, arrange your altar to Cybele. Place the image in the center back and then group the other items pleasingly around it. You may add other embellishments if you wish—more candles, more pine cones, elaborate and fancy dishes to hold the food and drink. It is appropriate to use your best.

Since you are directly petitioning a goddess rather than working a spell or performing a large ritual, you will not need to perform a quarter calling. It is not necessary to call upon deities other than the one you are petitioning.

Dress in whatever you will be comfortable to move in, at whatever level of movement you prefer. If you would like to wear elaborate dancing clothes or ritual wear, this is the time for it! Begin by turning off extra electronic devices and lights. Put yourself in a reflective frame of mind. You may start the music now.

Light the candle and incense if you are using it. Take a moment to center yourself. Say, "Cybele, goddess of the wild, goddess of loss and renewal, I (we) invite you to attend."

Pour the wine or fruit juice into the goblet, then pour a libation into the bowl and then sip from the goblet yourself. Say, "Thank you for sharing this cup with me."

Break the bread and put a piece in the food offerings bowl if you are using bread. If you are using nuts or mushrooms, put a piece in the food offerings bowl. Take a taste for yourself as well. Say, "Thank you for sharing this food with me."

Close your eyes and listen to the music. Imagine yourself in a forest glen with great trees rising around you. If you have a tambourine or other musical instrument, you may use it now. Think of how you want to experience renewal, what you want to leave behind and what you want to begin. Or, perhaps rather than imagining concrete things, simply feel the need to let go.

Let the music move you; let it twist around inside your heart. Begin to dance however you wish. You may simply sway in time to the music or engage in elaborate traditional choreography. Or you may go full out with club dancing! There is no right or wrong. Dance is physical expression. Simply express yourself in whatever way feels right to you. You may feel sad or elated; whatever you feel, let it flow. You are part of a tradition thousands of years old, dancing in honor of Cybele, goddess of the wild and of the wild at heart.

When you feel that you are finished, wind down your dance. Bow to the altar as if to an audience. Say, "Thank you, Cybele, for the privilege of joining your sacred train."

Turn off the music and put out the incense and the candles if you did this rite alone. The libation bowl should be emptied outdoors if possible. The remaining wine or juice in the glass should be consumed. You will want to ground and center with refreshments of some kind, at least with a liquid if not with a meal. If you are doing this rite with a group, you may like to have a meal together in the goddess's presence before blowing out the candles and putting out the incense so that you may share it with her.

When you are entirely finished, take down the altar. You may keep a pine cone as an emblem of your experience. Know that you are part of Cybele's mystery, even if you are not called as an initiate. You have experienced what people in the Hellenistic world did when they saw Cybele's sacred procession passing by and joined it, dancing behind the galli to the drums and tambourines.

Cybele's Correspondences

Here are some correspondences to help you honor Cybele, whether it's setting up an altar to her, planning a ritual that invokes her, or simply bringing some of her energy into your daily life.

Colors: Dark green, black

Incense: Pine, cedar, or fir

Symbols: Black stone, pine cone

Festival Day: Spring Equinox or the full moon of March

Food: Nuts, mushrooms, bread

Chapter Nine

Bringing It All Together

We began this book asking "Why the Hellenistic world?" Let's return to that question. Today, in a world which is increasingly socially fragmented, we need the broad, welcoming goddesses of the Hellenistic world. We need Aphrodite Pandemos, who says love is for everyone. We need Isis, the Mother of the World. We need Cybele, who welcomes all to her mysteries. We need a different model of a multi-cultural society.

Syncretism

Let's look at the differences between some concepts that are difficult for us to talk about. Colonialism is when a dominant people forces another people to change their culture and religion. If this book is sold in Germany, that is not colonialism. Nobody in Germany is being forced to read this book or change their religion in response. True colonialism is systemic and cruel. It is taking children away from their families, suppressing native languages and beliefs, and even killing people who continue to practice their traditional religions. To call any cultural sharing colonialism is to trivialize the impact of actual colonialism.

Cultural appropriation is taking the private, unsharable parts of another culture and using them out of context, particularly in a religious sense. It is not watching anime if you're not Japanese—things intended for sharing such as TV shows, which are gladly and joyfully shown to a global audience by their creators, are not cultural appropriation. It is not a violation of privacy to buy art a creator is selling to you. In fact it is supporting creators in that culture. Cultural appropriation is about consent. Taking something from a culture that people within that culture are trying to keep private is appropriation. If it is offered to you, it is not stolen.

The other issue is when someone from a dominant culture borrows from a smaller culture and then profits from it rather than the creators. For example, if someone finds a condiment in a culture little-known around the globe, creates a recipe for their version, and then markets it worldwide as the "authentic" thing and thereby pushing the original to the margins, this is likely cultural appropriation. However, someone from that culture bottling their recipe as a condiment assuredly isn't.

The other question we must ask is: It a living culture? It is at the very least horribly rude to proclaim yourself a member of a culture and then proceed to tell everyone what you think it should be when you have not had the experience of living in that culture for most of your life. Identity is deeper than feeling—it is also experience. People are generally offended by someone who has identified with a culture for a short time attempting to explain it.

Opposite to appropriation is syncretism, the coming together of more than one culture or tradition to make a hybrid in which all parties are willingly participating. For example, if you change any recipes of your grandmother's and put sriracha in it, that's syncretism. People and cultures grow and change, and it is natural for us to learn from one another. We see something being shared and like it so we adopt it, whether it's a recipe or a hairstyle or religious practice. It becomes part of our culture, just as rice became part of Hellenistic culture (see chapter one)—it was not because a king declared that everyone would eat rice or that rice was stolen from India, but because it was shared. People tried it and liked it.

In our world today, we may despair of how such disparate people can coexist. We may hopefully put a bumper sticker on our car that says "Coexist" and yet it seems impossible to achieve. However, the challenge of a suddenly wide and diverse world has been met before—by syncretism. And yes, that means that everyone changes. Nobody's recipe is the same as it was two hundred years ago. Younger people are adding sriracha and using the microwave to heat ingredients and frying things in olive oil instead of bacon grease or lard. But that's a choice: If you decide to make a recipe with heart-healthy olive oil instead of bacon grease, you are choosing to do so; you're not being forced to give up bacon grease, nor are you culturally appropriating olive oil from Mediterranean peoples. All the same, you are changing. You are altering tradition.

The change of tradition is where the conflict always lies in syncretism. People prefer anime or British rock or American movies or curries or tacos or whatever. "Inauthentic" dishes such as pizza become wildly popular. By the time I can order Thai barbecue pizza, we are truly talking about global syncretism!

There is always a tension between a culture's gatekeepers and people who are being syncretic. There will be a person who says, "that's not real art" and "you're doing it wrong." In our own cultures we usually are very aware of these currents. We know that Aunt Jenny won't like using olive oil instead of bacon grease. We know that certain people will say that a cooking technique isn't "authentic" if it isn't the way it was done a century ago. We are aware of internal cultural tensions and gauge them to make a decision (e.g., whether to use bacon grease or not). However, we don't usually know how to identify them in other cultures.

This same difficulty in identification of cultural differences is true of modes of worship as well as food. One reason for presenting the great goddesses of the Hellenistic world is that they are already syncretic. Long ago, they stopped being the gods of a place or a people and welcomed worshipers of any background. They already changed and welcome mutation.

Ultimately, history teaches us that syncretism happens. When people live together without physical barriers, they share. Sharing is human. Unless there are deliberate, sustained policies to keep people apart, they will come together. When they do, something new and amazing will be born.

Learning from the Great Goddesses of the Hellenistic World

Each of the goddesses in this book is already transformed. Each has already been adapted by diverse societies. Here are some questions to consider about the goddesses we have met:

- When you think of Isis as Mother of the World, what does that mean? How can we relate to her as a universal mother goddess? What can we learn from her stories?

- What does the spread of Atargatis's worship to people beyond her original location teach us? What does it say that we do not know the ethnicities of her worshipers?

- How are loss and renewal universal concepts? What can we learn from Cybele about them?

These are examples of specific questions to ask yourself now that you have read about each of them.

Now consider your broad reactions to all seven goddesses. Remember, in the Hellenistic World you probably would have been familiar with many of them at the same time. They were not exclusive but all part of a tapestry of worship.

- Which goddess's story spoke to you most? Why do you think that was?

- Which story surprised you most? What was surprising to you?

- Which story did you like least? Why is that? How did it challenge you?

- What did you think about the stories that involved historical figures? How do you relate the same or differently to stories of actual people, like Arsinoë or Themistocles?

- If you were going to tell a story of one of these goddesses, what would it be?

Take one of these questions as the basis of a journal entry. Make time and space to think and respond. Arrange a quiet moment, put on evocative music if you like, and truly consider your response.

A Deeper Connection

Now let's dive deeper: choose one goddess you have read about and seek out further information about her. Maybe it's a goddess who is well-known today, like Isis or Athena. If so, you may find it easy to discover many books and articles, including entire books that recreate her worship for modern pagans. If it's a goddess who is less well-known, like Atargatis, you may have a more challenging time. However, there are also many online resources. (I won't list them here because they are continually changing.) Here are some questions to consider about the goddess you have chosen to learn more about:

- Does she have different aspects from the ones shown in this book? How does learning about them deepen your understanding of her?

- What was her history before she became a great goddess of the Hellenistic world? How did her role change as her worshipers became more diverse?

- How was she seen after the Hellenistic period? For example, many of these goddesses were worshiped in the Roman world too. How did her worship change?

- How has she been seen in the years between the classical world and now? For example, some of these goddesses were iconic in later periods—Renaissance and Enlightenment versions of Aphrodite and Athena abound. How do those visions fit?

• How is this goddess seen today? Are there extensive modern reconstructions of her worship, or does she remain relatively obscure? If there are modern books devoted to her, how do they fit with your picture of her? Which books work for you and why?

The Journey Continues

As you seek to deepen your relationship with these ancient goddesses, I encourage you to seek additional resources. I have included a by-no-means exhaustive list of resources, but it is only a starting point for your research. There are many fine Neopagan and scholarly resources to consider. Remember that because of the breadth of these goddesses' worship over a long period of time, you may find disparate and contradictory information, which is to be expected. It is quite possible that all the things you find are right; they present snapshots of different places and times in what was a diverse and rich religious tradition. Remember, asking a question such as "How was Isis worshiped?" is like asking "How do Christians celebrate Christmas?" That's not a question that can be definitively answered even if you confine yourself to asking about the modern United States, much less all Christians everywhere in the world for the last thousand years! If you find contradictions or major differences, it is only to be expected.

Most resources fall into two categories, the first of which is scholarly information about a particular place and time. One can reasonably ask, "How was Cybele worshiped in Rome in the second century CE?" or "What do we know about the Temple of Isis at Pompeii based on archaeology?" These kinds of resources are the basis of much of what we know. (The other basis being surviving ancient texts.) However, they may or may not be helpful in creating a personal practice for you.

The second kind of resource is a modern reconstruction of worship intended for Neopagans. Again, there are some excellent books about several of these goddesses, making it easy to find one that speaks to you. If not, you can do as the authors have done and create rites and practices based on your own research to address aspects of the goddess that strike you as important or unique. If you are interested in a goddess who does not have large amounts of reconstructive material (such as Tyche or Atargatis) you can do your own research and create your own reconstructions.

Remember, the great goddesses of the Hellenistic world are already syncretic. They are not going to be offended if you use the wrong kind of incense or substitute vegan treats for their traditional offering. Syncretism is all about adaptation. There is absolutely nothing wrong with adding things that are meaningful to you or subtracting things that don't work today. For example, many of these goddesses originally received animal sacrifices. Obviously you are not going to kill a bull on an altar to any of them! It is certainly acceptable to make an offering of bread or fruit instead. While on your journey, be true to the spirit of the rite rather than to the exact recreation of ancient worship. We are not our ancestors; we are not even our grandparents. We are not defined by them, and all of these goddesses embrace that.

May their bright blessings be upon you.

Appendix

Helpful Charts

Here are some useful resources to help you use this book alone or with a group. As many ancient religions were practiced, you may wish to work through the entire book as a cycle with rites to different goddesses at appropriate times.

Dates for Rites and Celebrations

If you are interested in using this book to plan a monthly cycle of rites, either as a solitary or for a group, this is what that cycle might look like. It works through the seven goddesses over half a year, beginning in February and ending in August. Each person should do the meditation first and then the rite. If you wish, you may do the meditation on the dark moon and the rite on the full moon.

February 18, or the full moon of February—Atargatis

March 15, or the full moon of March—Cybele

April 11, or the full moon of April—Tyche

May 1, or the full moon of May—Aphrodite

June 13, or the full moon of June—Epona

July 23, or the full moon of July—Isis

August 1, or the full moon of August—Athena

If you are interested in using this book as a yearlong cycle rather than monthly, the following schedule begins with Imbolc, since many groups meet only on the eight quarters and cross-quarters It could also be used in a solitary practice.

Imbolc: Epona

Spring Equinox: Atargatis

Beltane: Aphrodite

Summer Solstice: Athena

Lammas: Isis

Fall Equinox: Tyche

Samhain: Cybele

Winter Solstice: All the goddesses together

The above order leads you logically through a cycle beginning with Epona, Lady of Horses, as the guardian of the flocks, then to Atargatis who expands the idea of guardianship as the Ruling Queen. Then we have Aphrodite at Beltane, Athena at Summer Solstice, and Isis at Lammas. Tyche comes to us on the cusp of Libra, and then Cybele, of death and rebirth, at Samhain. The

Winter Solstice can be a celebration or bring together all you have experienced using the last chapter to reflect on this amazing year.

Other Goddesses of the Hellenistic World

While we have examined seven of the most prominent goddesses worshiped in the Hellenistic world, there are many others to explore. Here are some examples.

Persephone/Proserpina—The Greek Queen of the Underworld, daughter of Demeter, wife of Hades, was widely worshiped across the Mediterranean. Known as Proserpina to the Romans, in the eastern part of the Hellenistic world she was often conflated with Isis in her role as Queen of the Dead.

Demeter/Ceres—The Greek mother goddess was conflated with the Roman Ceres, goddess of grain, and with Isis as Baubo in Egypt. Her worship was also widespread, usually in tandem with her daughter.

Nike—The goddess of victory was invoked across the Hellenistic world for prowess in battle. She was sometimes seen as an aspect of Athena, sometimes as a separate goddess.

Asherah—A Canaanite goddess of fertility and bounty, her worship continued in the Eastern Mediterranean throughout the Hellenistic period. She was often conflated with Isis or Aphrodite.

Selene—The personification of the moon, she was worshiped widely, often in tandem with her brother, Helios, the sun.

Bastet/Bast—The Egyptian cat goddess, she brings joy and fertility but also protects the home. She spread with cats from Egypt to the far corners of the world.

There are many other goddesses you will encounter if you read and research the Hellenistic period because there were literally hundreds of goddesses worshiped. Many were local or unique to a particular people and time rather than widespread, but all of them are fascinating!

Bibliography

Aeschylus. *The Persians*. Translated by Robert Potter. London: Routledge & Sons, 1932.

Barnes, Ian. *The Historical Atlas of the Celtic World*. New York: Chartwell, 2009.

BBC News. "Dig Reveals Roman Transvesite" *BBC News*. May 21, 2002. http://news.bbc.co.uk/2/hi/uk_news/england /1999734.stm.

Bernstein, Frances. *Classical Living: Reconnecting with the Rituals of Ancient Rome*. New York: HarperCollins, 2000.

Bilde, Per, ed. *Religion and Religious Practice in the Seleucid Kingdom*. Oxford, UK: Aarhus University Press, 1996.

Breitenberger, Barbara. *Aphrodite and Eros: The Development of Erotic Mythology in Early Greek Poetry and Cult*. New York: Routledge, 2007.

Carney, Elizabeth Donnelly. *Arsinoë of Egypt and Macedon: A Royal Life*. Oxford, UK: Oxford University Press, 2013.

Claus, Patricia. "New Findings on Santorini Point to Lost Island of Atlantis Origins" in *The Greek Reporter*, May 2021. https://greekreporter.com/2021/05/21/new-findings-on-santorini-point-to-lost-island-of-atlantis-origins/.

Cook, P. D. MacKenzie. *Epona: Hidden Goddess of the Celts*. London: Avalonia Press, 2016.

Diodorus of Sicily. *The Library of History Book II*. Translated by C. Bedford Welles. Cambridge, MA: Harvard University Press, 1963.

Empereur, Jean-Yves. *Alexandria: Jewel of Egypt*. Translated by Jane Brenton. New York: Thames & Hudson, 2001.

Grant, Michael. *From Alexander to Cleopatra: The Hellenistic World*. New York: Scribner and Sons, 1982.

Green, Peter. *Alexander to Actium: The Historical Evolution of the Hellenistic Age*. Berkeley, CA: University of California Press, 1990.

Gurewitsch, Matthew. "True Colors." *Smithsonian Magazine*. July 2008. https://www.smithsonianmag.com/arts-culture/true-colors-17888/.

Hughes, Bettany. *Venus and Aphrodite: A Biography of Desire*. New York: Basic Books, 2020.

keegan1234. "Cybele, the Mother Goddess." *Women in Antiquity* (blog). November 2018. https://womeninantiquity.wordpress.com/2018/11/27/cybele-the-mother-goddess.

Lucian. *The Syrian Goddess: de Dea Syria*. Translated by Herbert A. Strong and John Garstang. Rookhope, UK: Aziloth Books, 2014.

Jones, Prudence, and Nigel Pennick. *A History of Pagan Europe*. New York: Barnes and Noble Books, 1995.

Kraemer, Ross S., ed. *Maenads, Martyrs, Matrons and Monastics: A Sourcebook on Women's Religions in the Greco-Roman World*. Philadelphia: Fortress Press, 1988.

Meredith, Jane. *Aphrodite's Magic*. Winchester, UK: O Books, 2010.

Monaghan, Patricia. *The Goddess Path: Myths, Invocations, and Rituals*. St. Paul, MN: Llewellyn Publications, 1999.

Museum of Classical Archaeology Databases. "Tyche of Antioch." Retrieved January 6, 2021. https://museum.classics.cam.ac.uk/collections/casts/tyche-antioch.

Pollard, Justin, and Howard Reid. *The Rise and Fall of Alexandria: Birthplace of the Modern Mind*. New York: Viking, 2006.

Pomeroy, Sarah B. *Women in Hellenistic Egypt: From Alexander to Cleopatra*. Detroit: Wayne State University Press, 1984.

Ratcliffe, Susan. *Concise Oxford Dictionary of Quotations*. Oxford, UK: Oxford Publishing, 2011.

Raven, Gwion. *The Magick of Food: Rituals, Offerings, and Why We Eat Together*. Woodbury, MN: Llewellyn Publications, 2020.

Reed, Ellen Cannon. *Circle of Isis: Ancient Egyptian Magic for Modern Witches*. Franklin Lakes, NJ: New Page Books, 2002.

Regula, DeTraci. *The Mysteries of Isis: Her Worship & Magick*. St. Paul, MN: Llewellyn Publications, 1996.

Reif, Jennifer. *Mysteries of Demeter: Rebirth of the Pagan Way*. York Beach, ME: Samuel Weiser, 1999.

Roux, Georges. *Ancient Iraq*. New York: Penguin, 1992.

Saunders, Nicholas J. *Alexander's Tomb: The Two-thousand-year Obsession to Find the Lost Conqueror*. New York: Basic Books, 2006.

Shepherd, William. *Salamis 480 BC: The Naval Campaign That Saved Greece*. Oxford, UK: Osprey Publishing, 2010.

Shipley, Graham. *The Greek World After Alexander 323–30 BC*. London: Routledge Taylor and Francis Group, 2000.

Sophia. *The Ultimate Guide to Goddess Empowerment*. Kansas City, KS: Andrews McMeel Publishing, 2003.

Strauss, Barry. *The Battle of Salamis: The Naval Encounter That Saved Greece*. New York: Simon and Schuster, 2004.

Telesco, Patricia. *365 Goddess: A Daily Guide to the Magic and Inspiration of the Goddess*. New York: HarperCollins, 1998.

Teixidor, Javier. "Interpretations and Misinterpretations of the East in Hellenistic Times." In *Religion and Religious Practice in the Seleucid Kingdom*. Oxford, UK: Aarhus University Press, 1990.

Trobe, Kala. *Invoke the Goddess: Connecting to the Hindu, Greek & Egyptian Deities*. Woodbury, MN: Llewellyn Publications, 2019.

Turcan, Robert. *The Cults of the Roman Empire*. Translated by Antonia Nevill. Oxford, UK: Blackwell Publishers, 1996.

Winter, Sarah Kate Istra. *Kharis: Hellenic Polytheism Explored*. Seattle: Amazon Digital Services LLC, 2008.

Zahle, Jan. "Religious Motifs on Seleucid Coins." In *Religion and Religious Practice in the Seleucid Kingdom*. Oxford, UK: Aarhus University Press, 1990.

To Write to the Author

If you wish to contact the author or would like more information about this book, please write to the author in care of Llewellyn Worldwide Ltd. and we will forward your request. Both the author and publisher appreciate hearing from you and learning of your enjoyment of this book and how it has helped you. Llewellyn Worldwide Ltd. cannot guarantee that every letter written to the author can be answered, but all will be forwarded. Please write to:

Jo Graham
℅ Llewellyn Worldwide
2143 Wooddale Drive
Woodbury, MN 55125-2989

Please enclose a self-addressed stamped envelope for reply,
or $1.00 to cover costs. If outside the U.S.A., enclose
an international postal reply coupon.

Many of Llewellyn's authors have websites with additional information and resources. For more information, please visit our website at http://www.llewellyn.com